DEVELOPING AGRICULTURE AND TOURISM FOR INCLUSIVE GROWTH IN THE LAO PEOPLE'S DEMOCRATIC REPUBLIC

SEPTEMBER 2021

ASIAN DEVELOPMENT BANK

ADB

Notes:
In this publication, "$" refers to United States dollars.
ADB recognizes "China" as the People's Republic of China; "Laos" and "Lao" as the Lao People's
Democratic Republic; "Vietnam" as Viet Nam; and "Hanoi" as Ha Noi.

On the cover: Clockwise from left: Weaver in Nongping Village (photo by Gerhard Joren); Patuxay
arch in central Vientiane. Patu means Door and xay means Victory (photo by Souphavanh
Phonmany); Organic vegetable farmer in Boung Phao Village (photo by Ariel Javellana); coffee
beans being grown in Pak Xong (photo by Gerhard Joren); High quality cabbage from Kongtoun
Village, Champasak Province (photo by Xaykhame Manilasit); a Lao airline, ART 72 at Pakxe
Airport (photo by Gerhard Joren).

Cover design by Michael Cortes.

Contents

Tables, Figures, and Boxes

Tables

Figures

Boxes

Foreword

Over the last 3 decades, the Lao People's Democratic Republic (Lao PDR) has witnessed remarkable growth, with its gross domestic product increasing at an average rate of 7% annually. However, growth has relied heavily on capital-intensive use of the country's abundant natural resources and created limited job opportunities. As a result, the pace of poverty reduction has become slow while inequality has widened. With most of the poor still relying on rural agriculture for their livelihood, a more productive agriculture sector and new opportunities through tourism can help reduce poverty and achieve inclusive growth. This report analyzes the Lao PDR's development achievements and discusses policy recommendations for further development of the agriculture and tourism sectors.

The Lao PDR has abundant fertile land and a relatively small population. Its geographic and climatic diversity is favorable for producing a wide variety of agricultural products. Although agricultural productivity has remained low largely due to limited use of chemical inputs, this apparent limitation can be turned into an advantage. Consumers in neighboring countries consider Lao agricultural products clean and safe. Thus, this study recommends promotion of organic farming for exports and local consumption, including by tourism enterprises. The study underscores much-needed investments in irrigation, research, and extension, to improve agricultural productivity.

The Lao PDR's rich cultural heritage and natural beauty have drawn an increasing number of visitors in recent years. Unfortunately, the ongoing coronavirus (COVID-19) pandemic has put a stop to travel and tourism. The survey of tourism enterprises conducted for this study in 2020 indicated that half of the tourism enterprises were temporarily closed. International tourism will become even more competitive once the pandemic subsides. People all over the world are waiting to travel, visit exotic destinations, experience new cultures, explore natural wonders, and savor different types of local cuisine. To ensure that the Lao PDR remains a competitive destination once international borders reopen, the study recommends continued investments in tourism infrastructure and human capital to deliver high-quality services, as prioritized in the government's medium-term development plan.

This report has been produced through close collaboration of the Government of the Lao PDR and the Asian Development Bank. We hope this study will continue to generate dialogue and provide meaningful input for the Lao PDR's plans and strategies in the post-pandemic era. The Lao PDR and ADB look forward to continued partnership and collaboration toward inclusive and sustainable development.

Phonevanh Outhavong
Deputy Minister
Ministry of Planning and Investment
Government of the
Lao People's Democratic Republic

Joseph E. Zveglich, Jr
Officer-in-Charge
Economic Research and Regional
Cooperation Department
Asian Development Bank

Acknowledgments

Developing Agriculture and Tourism for Inclusive Growth in the Lao People's Democratic Republic was prepared by the Asian Development Bank (ADB) under the regional technical assistance project (RETA 8343), Country Diagnostic Studies in Selected Developing Member Countries. This study was undertaken by the Economic Research and Regional Cooperation Department (ERCD) of the ADB. Former directors of the Economic Analysis and Operational Support Division (EREA) guided its preparation—initially, Edimon Ginting who is now country director at the Bangladesh Resident Mission of ADB's South Asia Department (SARD) and, thereafter, Rana Hasan who is now regional economic advisor at the Office of the Director General of SARD. The study was completed under the supervision of EREA Director Lei Lei Song. Takashi Yamano and Manisha Pradhananga led the study, with Jindra Nuella Samson and Lotis Quiao providing overall research and technical assistance. Steven Schipani, Southeast Asia Department, shared his experience and expertise, and was an integral part of the study team. Aileen Roxas Gatson and Gee Ann Carol D. Burac provided administration support.

Buakhai Phimmavong and her team from Enterprise & Development Consultants Co., Ltd. conducted the survey of tourism enterprises under the supervision of the study team. Kym Anderson and Josef Yap provided overall technical review and economic editing, with support from Tuesday Soriano as copyeditor. Reneli Ann Gloria, Angelica Maddawin, and Daryll Naval provided research and data assistance. Mike Cortes did the graphic design and layout.

We are grateful to the Luxembourg Development Cooperation Agency for generously sharing data from their 2018 survey of tourism enterprises.

We would like to thank ADB's Lao People's Democratic Republic (Lao PDR) Resident Mission for their generous support and invaluable comments, particularly Sonomi Tanaka, country director; Yasushi Negishi, former country director; Emma R. Allen, country economist; and Soulinthone Leuangkhamsing, senior economics officer.

This study benefited from invaluable comments received from peer reviewers including Omer Zafar, principal natural resource and agriculture specialist, Lao PDR Resident Mission; Phoxay Xayyavong, senior social sector officer, Lao PDR Resident Mission; Leonard Leung, natural resources and agriculture economist, Southeast Asia Department; and Mark Bezuijen, principal environment specialist, East Asia Department. We thank ADB's Department of Communications for final review and support in printing and web publication.

This study is a product of extensive consultations with key government ministries in the Lao PDR and their agencies. We are especially grateful to Xaysomphet Norasingh, director general, Department of Trade and Promotion, Ministry of Industry and Commerce; Sitthiroth Rasphone, head of the Center for Development Policy Research, Ministry of Planning and Investment (MPI); Latdavanh Songvilay, acting director general, Center for Macroeconomic Policy and Economic Restructuring, National Institute for Economic Research; Phonemaly Inthaphome, deputy director general, Tourism Development Department and project manager of the Second Greater Mekong Subregion Tourism Infrastructure for Inclusive Growth, Ministry of Information, Culture and Tourism; and Kalouna Nanthavongduangsy, deputy director general, Planning Department, MPI for their invaluable guidance and support to the study, including a thorough review of final report.

We would also like to thank the Champasak Department of Information, Culture, and Tourism Office and Information Center; Champasak Provincial Agriculture and Forestry Office; Louangphabang Department of Information, Culture, and Tourism Office; Louangphabang Provincial Agriculture and Forestry Office; and Khone District Tourism Office for their valuable insights and coordination of field visit and meetings with various stakeholder groups.

Last, we would like to extend our thanks to external stakeholders and partners including the World Bank, International Finance Corporation, Australian Centre for International Agricultural Research, Paksong Lao–China Agriculture Cooperation Center, and various agricultural farmer groups; Nakasang Boat Operators, Guesthouse, and Market Associations; Khone Phapheng Waterfall Park; Nam Pa Irrigation Subproject Office; Lao National Chambers of Commerce and Industry; and the Destination Management Network Offices in Pakxe and Louangphabang whose insights have been instrumental to the study.

Author Profiles

Kym Anderson is a George Gollin professor emeritus at the School of Economics of the University of Adelaide (where he has been affiliated since 1984) and an honorary professor at the Australian National University's Crawford School of Public Policy (where he was a research fellow in 1977–1983 and a part-time professor of economics in 2012–2018). During two periods of extended leave he served as deputy head of economic research at the General Agreement on Tariffs and Trade (now World Trade Organization) secretariat in Geneva (1990–1992) and as lead economist (Trade Policy) at the World Bank in Washington, DC (2004–2007). In 2010–2017, he served on the Board of Trustees of the International Food Policy Research Institute in Washington, DC, chairing it from 2015. Since doctoral studies at the University of Chicago and Stanford University, he has published more than 400 articles and 40 books. He is a recipient of an honorary doctor of economics degree from the University of Adelaide and a distinguished alumni award from the University of New England. In 2015, he became a Companion of the Order of Australia (AC).

Soulinthone Leuangkhamsing is a senior economics officer at the Lao People's Democratic Republic (Lao PDR) Resident Mission of the Asian Development Bank (ADB). Before joining ADB in 2008, he was an economist at the Lao PDR Resident Representative Office of the International Monetary Fund. He participated in the preparation of the Asian Development Outlook's Lao chapter, annual country programming, and country partnership strategy. He also supported the processing and implementation of the governance and public finance management programs. He holds a master's degree in business administration from the School of Management of the Asian Institute of Technology in Thailand and a bachelor of economics from Flinders University of South Australia.

Manisha Pradhananga is an economist at the Economic Research and Regional Cooperation Department (ERCD) of ADB. She joined ADB in 2018. Before that, Manisha was an assistant professor of economics at Knox

College, United States (US) where she taught courses in macroeconomics, international trade, and economic development. In 2011–2013, she worked at the ADB Institute in Japan as a research associate. Manisha obtained her PhD in economics from the University of Massachusetts, Amherst and bachelor's degree from Mount Holyoke College, US.

Jindra Nuella Samson is a senior economics officer at ERCD of ADB. She has been with ADB for over 12 years, contributing to various analytical research on agricultural and natural resources, climate change, economic analyses, and country diagnostics studies. Before ADB, she was an assistant scientist and resource economist at the International Center for Tropical Agriculture, stationed at the International Rice Research Institute in Los Baños, Philippines. She worked earlier as a researcher in various nongovernment organizations conducting environmental impact assessments in the Philippines. She obtained her master's degree in environmental science and bachelor's degree in development economics from the University of the Philippines.

Steven Schipani is a principal tourism industry specialist at the Southeast Asia Department of ADB and based in the Lao PDR. He also leads ADB's tourism support program in the Greater Mekong Subregion. A US national, Steven has worked in Southeast Asia for more than 25 years, starting his career as a US peace corps volunteer in Thailand. He holds a master's degree in public health from Emory University and a bachelor's degree in public health from Southern Connecticut State University.

Lotis Quiao is an economics officer at ERCD of ADB. She has been involved in the department's work for 7 years, reviewing economic analyses of energy projects, preparing power sector assessments, and other analytical work pertaining to country diagnostic studies. Before joining ADB, she was a consultant at the World Bank. She has a master's degree in development economics from the University of the Philippines.

Takashi Yamano is a principal economist at ERCD of ADB. His current responsibilities include economic research and conducting reviews of project economic analyses. Before joining ADB in 2017, he was an impact assessment specialist at the International Rice Research Institute from 2011 to 2017. In 2002–2011, he was a professor at the National Graduate Institute for Policy Studies in Tokyo, Japan. In 2000–2002, he was a consultant at the World Bank in Washington, DC. He obtained a joint PhD in economics and agricultural economics at Michigan State University in 2000.

Josef T. Yap was president of the Philippine Institute for Development Studies (PIDS), where he worked for 26 years until his retirement on 30 June 2013. While at PIDS, he specialized in macroeconomic policy and applied econometrics. He finished his undergraduate and doctoral studies at the University of the Philippines (UP) Diliman and then took a post-graduate program at the University of Pennsylvania. In 2010, he was honored as one of the 100 outstanding alumni of the UP Diliman College of Engineering. His current research interests center on regional economic integration in East Asia and promoting energy security in the Philippines. Josef was the regional coordinator of the East Asian Development Network and played an active role in the establishment of the Economic Research Institute for ASEAN and East Asia. He is currently a senior technical advisor to the Access to Sustainable Energy Programme – Clean Energy Living Laboratories (ASEP-CELLs) project, which is being implemented under the auspices of the European Union and the Ateneo School of Government.

Executive Summary

In the last 3 decades, the Lao People's Democratic Republic (Lao PDR) has experienced remarkable economic growth, quadrupling per capita income from $445 in 1989 to $1,840 in 2019 in constant 2010 dollar terms. Although there was a marked decline in the share of people below the national poverty line, it was accompanied by rising inequality. The GINI coefficient increased from 31.0 in 1993 to 38.8 in 2019. An earlier ADB study identified the tremendous potential for developing the agriculture and tourism sectors to achieve inclusive growth.

The Lao PDR is endowed with extensive land, has a relatively small population, and is surrounded by rapidly growing economies. But the country's agricultural productivity remains low. Currently, the agriculture sector employs over 60% of the labor force and supports the livelihood of rural households. Given its abundant natural resources and rich cultural heritage, tourism has emerged as a potential sector with strong backward linkages. Until the onset of the coronavirus disease (COVID-19) pandemic in 2020, the Lao PDR's tourism sector had been expanding rapidly. This report develops a framework to examine potential linkages between the agriculture and tourism sectors and emphasizes the need to develop synergies between them for an inclusive post-pandemic recovery.

The country's geographic and climatic diversity is favorable for producing a wide variety of agricultural products. Chapter 2 discusses in detail the pattern of agricultural production across provinces and regions. After a long period of subsistence farming, agricultural production in the Lao PDR has become more market-oriented and diversified in the last few decades. Although rice used to be a dominant crop, it now covers only half of the cropland and contributes 20% of the total agricultural value production. The shares of vegetable and livestock production values are both at 20% and are expected to grow more. The challenge is to identify and establish value chains for vegetables and livestock. Tourism enterprises could be part of these value chains as they provide high-quality and high-value products to domestic and international tourists.

Chapter 3 provides an overview of tourism in the Lao PDR in the context of global and regional tourism. Before the onset of the COVID-19 pandemic, global tourism was a rapidly growing industry. International tourist arrivals worldwide reached 1.5 billion in 2019. As foreign tourist arrivals in the Lao PDR rose from 2.5 million in 2010 to 4.1 million in 2018, contributing 12% of the country's gross domestic product (GDP), the government declared 2018 as "Visit Laos Year"; arrivals further increased to 4.8 million the following year. Lao tourism thrived on visitors mainly from Southeast Asian countries, which accounted for 67% of international arrivals in 2019. About 63% of international tourists mentioned cultural attractions as the main reason for their visit. In 2019, international tourism receipts totaling about $935 million became a main source of foreign exchange earnings. But the average spending per international tourist was less than $200, the lowest in Southeast Asia. Clearly, additional investments are needed to upgrade the country's tourism infrastructure and attract high-spending tourists. The tourism sector employed an estimated 42,000 workers, 62% of whom were women. In 2018, there were about 1,400 unfilled tourism jobs, which indicates a need for skilled workers in the sector.

To examine employment in tourism enterprises and the impact of the COVID-19 pandemic, the Asian Development Bank conducted surveys of tourism enterprises in four popular tourism destinations in the country. Chapter 4 describes the four destinations and discusses the survey results. More than 360 tourism enterprises, such as hotels and restaurants, participated in the 2019 and 2020 surveys. The 2019 survey questions related to employment and links with the agriculture industry. Tourism enterprises spent a large share of food expenditure on imported seafood, meat, and local fish. A significant share of these enterprises purchased local organic vegetables, and about 60% of them advertised their use of organic vegetables. The 2020 follow-up survey assessed the impacts of the COVID-19 pandemic. The survey showed that half of the tourism enterprises temporarily closed in May 2020, and about 70% of them had reduced their number of workers, with employee numbers falling by 38%. The negative impact was larger among enterprises that had targeted international guests before 2020.

Finally, Chapter 5 presents policy recommendations to foster inclusive growth through agriculture and tourism. Proposed immediate and short-term responses to the COVID-19 pandemic include the following: providing financial assistance to tourism enterprises, accelerating the national COVID-19 vaccination program, enabling the responsible restart of travel and tourism, and adopting transparent, effective, and clearly communicated health and safety protocols. Over the medium and long term, the Lao PDR must seek to raise the competitiveness of its agriculture and tourism sectors, while strengthening the linkages between them. It must also invest in much-needed physical infrastructure in transport, irrigation, urban services, and digital connectivity as well as develop human capital, expand visa exemptions, and foster organic food production and certification. These investments and policy reforms will ensure a rapid post-pandemic recovery, while moving the Lao PDR closer to inclusive growth.

Abbreviations

ADB	Asian Development Bank
ADS	Agricultural Development Strategy
ASEAN	Association of Southeast Asian Nations
ESS	Enterprise Survey of Employment and Skills
FAO	Food and Agriculture Organization of the United Nations
FDI	foreign direct investment
GDP	gross domestic product
GMS	Greater Mekong Subregion
ha	hectare
km	kilometer
Lao PDR	Lao People's Democratic Republic
LANITH	Lao National Institute for Tourism and Hospitality
MICT	Ministry of Information, Culture and Tourism
NEM	New Economic Mechanism
NSEDP	National Socioeconomic Development Plan
PGS	participatory guarantee system
PRC	People's Republic of China
RD&E	research, development, and extension
SDG	Sustainable Development Goal
SMEs	small and medium-sized enterprises
UN	United Nations
UNESCO	United Nations Educational, Scientific and Cultural Organization
UNWTO	United Nations World Tourism Organization
US	United States
WFP	World Food Programme
WTTC	World Travel & Tourism Council

CHAPTER 1

Ensuring Inclusive Growth in Navigating Growth in the Lao PDR

Kym Anderson, Takashi Yamano, Jindra Samson, Soulinthone Leuangkhamsing, and Josef Yap

Introduction

The Lao People's Democratic Republic (Lao PDR) is a country with 7,275,560 people (UNDESA 2019) living in an area of approximately 23 million hectares. It is landlocked to the north by the People's Republic of China (PRC), to the south by Cambodia, to the east by Viet Nam, to the northwest by Myanmar, and to the west by Thailand. The country has experienced rapid economic growth in recent years, but this expansion depended heavily on its abundant natural minerals. An earlier diagnostic report of the country's economy noted the tremendous potential for developing its agriculture and services sectors and highlighted the importance of strengthening synergies across various sectors to achieve inclusive growth (ADB 2017a).[1] This report describes the economic success of the Lao PDR over the past 3 decades and the current efforts to sustain and build upon these gains. It focuses on the potential benefits from agriculture and tourism, particularly resulting from strengthening linkage between the two sectors.

Although smaller in size than its neighbors, the Lao PDR has ample room for strong inclusive economic growth through the development of its agriculture sector. The country is endowed with extensive land, has a relatively small population, and is surrounded by rapidly growing economies. The potential demand from neighboring countries for Lao agricultural products is large and expected to grow. But the country's agricultural productivity remains low and its current agricultural exports to neighboring countries limited.

---

[1] Inclusive growth can be defined narrowly, with a focus on economic growth, or broadly, with emphasis on non-income measures of well-being and valuing human capabilities, as discussed in McKinley (2010). This report takes a narrow focus on economic growth with a declining income inequality through development of the agriculture and tourism sectors in the country.

Tourism is another sector recognized for its potential in contributing to inclusive growth. The Lao PDR has witnessed a rapid rise in international tourists, although their level of spending is low compared with tourism spending in neighboring countries. A higher level of per tourist expenditure is needed to benefit the local economy and achieve sustainable and inclusive tourism.

Three Decades of Economic Growth and Structural Change in the Lao PDR

Since the introduction of the New Economic Mechanism (NEM) in 1986, the Lao PDR's economy has grown rapidly. Under NEM, the government introduced various economic and structural reforms to reduce price and production controls, allow private investment, and attract foreign direct investment (FDI). Gross domestic product (GDP) rose sixfold and averaged 7.2% growth per year in 2000–2019. The average per capita income in constant 2010 prices increased from $440 in 1986 to $1,840 in 2019.[2] Associated with this rapid growth was a marked decline in the share of people below the national poverty line—from 46% in 1993 to 23% in 2012. However, poverty reduction has been uneven between urban and rural areas, as well as across provinces. Between 2013 and 2019, achievement in poverty reduction in rural areas has been more evident, where it significantly dropped from 31% in 2013 to 24% in 2019 compared with urban areas where poverty rates remained at 7% in both periods. The northern region, once considered to be the poorest of all regions has also made impressive progress in reducing poverty, while many provinces too in the southern region exhibited catch-up due to rapid decline in poverty (World Bank 2020).

Major structural changes accompanied these remarkable achievements. The economy has become far more open, with trade's share of GDP rising from an average of 11% in 1984–1986 to 87% in 2015–2016. The contribution of agriculture to GDP, on the other hand, fell by almost two-thirds, from 46% in 1989–1991 to 18% in 2015–2017. Employment in agriculture, however, has remained relatively high, declining from above 85% before 1995 to 60% of total employment in 2018.

Agriculture still accounts for the majority of Lao PDR jobs, averaging 62% of the workforce in 2017–2019, but dropping from 86% in 1991–1993 (Table 1.1). However, agriculture's share of GDP is low at only 16% in

---

[2]   The World Bank. Lao PDR Data. https://data.worldbank.org/country/LA (accessed 31 October 2020).

2017–2019, considerably lower from 46% in 1991–1993. In contrast, the manufacturing sector's GDP share is almost three times its employment share. The same can be seen for services in 1991–1993. This implies that farm workers are far less productive than nonfarm workers, especially those in mining and manufacturing.

Table 1.1: Lao PDR Sectoral Shares of Employment and GDP, 1991–2019
(%)

Employment	1991–1993	2017–2019
Agriculture	86	62
Industry	3	13
Services	11	25
Total	100	100
GDP	**1991–1993**	**2017–2019**
Agriculture	46	16
Industry	12	40
Services	42	44
Total	100	100

GDP = gross domestic product, Lao PDR = Lao People's Democratic Republic.
Sources: World Development Indicators (accessed January 2021); Lao Statistics Bureau for GDP shares 2017 to 2019 (accessed January 2021).

Agricultural products are major export products, although their importance has declined in recent years. In 2010–2016, food and agriculture accounted for 20% of all exported goods and services, a decline from a share of 33% in 1991–1993. Over the same period, the shares of mining (mostly copper and electricity) drastically increased from 8% to 42%, and tourism increased its export value from a negligible level to 18%. On the other hand, the share of manufacturing in total exports declined from 29% in 1991–1993 to 15% in 2010–2016.

The country's export indexes of revealed comparative advantage,[3] shown in the right-hand column of Table 1.2 suggests that the country is still most competitive globally in primary production. Within the primary sector, the export prices of timber, copper, and electricity relative to other export products strongly influence how competitive Lao PDR farmers can be in international markets.

---

[3] Revealed comparative advantage is defined as the share of a sector in Lao PDR exports of goods and services divided by that sector's share of global exports.

Table 1.2: Lao PDR Exports, 1991–2016
(%)

Exports	1991–1993	2010–2016	RCA[a]
Food	4	16	(2.3)
Other agriculture	29	4	(3.0)
Mining	8	42	(2.9)
Copper	0	26	
Electricity	8	15	
Other	0	1	
Manufacturing	29	15	(0.3)
Services	30	23	(1.1)
Tourism	NA	18	
Other services	NA	5	
Total	**100**	**100**	**(1.0)**

( ) = negative, Lao PDR = Lao People's Democratic Republic, NA = not applicable, RCA = revealed comparative advantage.
[a] RCA is the *revealed* comparative index of Balassa (1965), defined as the share of a sector in Lao PDR exports of goods and services divided by that sector's share of global exports in 2010–2016.
Sources: Bank of the Lao PDR Annual Reports (various issues); and World Bank (2020).

Opening up of the economy has also spurred an influx of visitors eager to see the once-closed country. Apart from its strategic location in the world's most populous region, the Lao PDR is endowed with outstanding tourism resources. The Ministry of Information, Culture and Tourism (MICT) recognizes 2,199 tourist sites as of 2019, of which 60% are categorized natural, 27% cultural, and 13% historic. These include a network of 33 national protected areas covering about 17% of the country, 3 United Nations Educational, Scientific and Cultural Organization (UNESCO) World Heritage sites, an Association of Southeast Asian Nations (ASEAN) Heritage Park, and many interesting cultural industries.[4] The Mekong River runs through 1,898 kilometers (km) of the Lao PDR's stunning mountain landscapes and forms the world's third largest waterfall by flow rate as it crashes over a 21-meter fault line near the border with Cambodia.

The growth of international tourist arrivals has varied in recent years. The number of international tourists nearly doubled from 2.5 million in 2010 to 4.7 million in 2015 (Table 1.3). After short-term declines in 2016 and 2017, the government and the private sector responded by organizing the "Visit Laos Year" 2018 program which helped increase arrivals by 8.3% to 4.2 million

---

[4]   UNESCO World Heritage sites include (i) the Town of Louangphabang, (ii) Vat Phou and Associated Ancient Settlements within the Champasak Cultural Landscape, and (iii) Megalithic Jar Sites in Xiangkhouang – Plain of Jars. Cultural industries comprise a range of economic activities concerned with generating of knowledge and information for cultural development such as architecture, art, crafts, design, fashion, film, music, performing arts, etc.

in 2018. Nevertheless, the Lao PDR's 2010–2018 cumulative annual growth rate fell to 5.3%, which significantly lags behind Southeast Asia's 6.9% annual growth rate during this period. While international arrivals continued upward to reach about 4.8 million in 2019, the Lao PDR like other destinations worldwide has witnessed a significant decline in 2020 because of the COVID-19 pandemic.

Table 1.3: Lao PDR International Tourist Arrivals, 2010–2019

Year	International Tourist Arrivals (million)	Year-on-Year Change (%)	Share of Southeast Asia International Tourist Arrivals (%)
2010	2.5	25.5	3.4
2011	2.7	8.8	3.3
2012	3.3	22.0	3.7
2013	3.8	13.2	3.6
2014	4.2	10.1	4.0
2015	4.7	12.8	4.3
2016	4.2	(9.6)	3.6
2017	3.9	(8.7)	3.0
2018	4.2	8.3	3.0
2019	4.8	14.4	3.3

( ) = negative, Lao PDR = Lao People's Democratic Republic.
Sources: MICT (2019); and ASEAN Secretariat.

According to MICT, international tourism receipts increased from $641.6 million in 2014 to 934.7 million in 2019. Tourism's direct contribution to GDP was 5.1% and total contribution about 10% in 2019 (see Chapter 3). International tourist spending is among the Lao PDR's main sources of foreign exchange, trailing mineral exports (about $1.4 billion), receipts from other industries (more than $1.2 billion), and electricity exports ($1.3 billion). However, receipts per international tourist average only $195.1, the lowest in Southeast Asia and significantly lower than Asia and the Pacific's $1,220 benchmark. It is estimated that tourism in the Lao PDR directly sustains 348,700 jobs, including travel, accommodation, and retail enterprises (WTTC 2021).

The Asian Development Bank (ADB) 2017 country diagnostic study for the Lao PDR identified both agriculture and tourism to have considerable potential for inclusive growth (ADB 2017a). These important sectors provide jobs in remote areas and can support each other in two ways: (i) the demand for high-quality agricultural products by tourism enterprises can be provided by local farmers; and (ii) the tourism sector can create opportunities for employment outside of the agriculture sector, thus boosting off-farm earnings of rural households. Before examining market and policy developments in the Lao PDR agriculture and tourism sectors, the next section draws on economic reasoning to outline the determinants of sectoral competitiveness in a natural resource–rich developing economy. A framework that links agriculture and tourism is presented thereafter with emphasis on the contribution of agritourism to inclusive and sustainable development.

Sectoral Competitiveness in a Resource-Rich Developing Economy

Most countries begin the process of economic transformation with the vast majority of people engaged in producing staple food, as did the Lao PDR (ADB 2020a). As labor productivity improves with the accumulation or importation of industrial capital, an increasing number of workers are absorbed by the manufacturing and services sectors. This leads to a decline in the absolute number and share of the population employed in agriculture. The increase in manufacturing jobs enables less-developed economies to supply the world with manufactures, especially those that are labor-intensive to produce. Economies that are rich in minerals, like the Lao PDR, generally employ many workers in the mining industry. Mining, however, tends to be capital-intensive; thus, its share of employment is not robust enough to sustain long-term jobs for the population.

Sectoral shares in GDP and in employment generally follow a similar pattern. However, the GDP share of agriculture often declines faster than its employment share, as in the Lao PDR. In contrast, the GDP shares of mining and manufacturing often decline slower than their employment shares, implying that labor productivity in these two sectors grows faster than the national average. Such labor productivity differences mean that, at the margin, migration of labor from traditional agriculture to manufacturing will likely accelerate economic growth. There is a tendency for services' share of GDP to grow slower than its share of employment because it (like traditional agriculture) is labor intensive, and productivity growth is relatively slow.

While this pattern of structural transformation has been taking place in the course of national economic growth for many decades, the pace of these sectoral changes varies widely across countries, and not only because of their different rates of economic growth.[5] Far more varied across countries

---

[5]   There is also structural transformation *within* sectors as growth proceeds. See, for example, Laborde et al. (2018) on agricultural transformation patterns.

are developments in the sectoral shares of national exports. Some of the world's highest-income countries have managed to retain a comparative advantage in a small number of primary products, while some low-income countries have already built a comparative advantage in one or more services. As part of the current wave of globalization, the further lowering of trade costs and government restrictions on trade, along with the digital revolution, are accelerating the fragmentation of production processes. This is making an ever-higher proportion of goods and services internationally tradable and changes in comparative advantage less predictable (Baldwin 2016, 2019; Constantinescu, Mattoo, and Ruta 2018; Rodrik 2018).

There are numerous explanations for the differences in the structural transformation patterns across countries. Commonly mentioned are differential rates of technological improvements (since multifactor productivity growth rates differ across sectors and in their factor-saving bias), rates of change in relative factor endowments (since factor intensities of production vary across sectors), and international terms of trade (since countries differ in their comparative advantages). Less-commonly considered are demand considerations; yet, per capita incomes matter because income and price elasticities of demand differ across sectors' products, including nontradables. Also important are policies that unequally distort consumer prices of the products of each sector.

A recent paper (Anderson and Ponnusamy 2019) uses data, for the 25 years to 2014, from 117 countries to show the extent to which declines in the relative importance of primary and then manufacturing sectors in GDP, employment, and exports are explained by changes in per capita income, relative factor endowments and, in the case of agriculture, the sector's own productivity growth. The results are unsurprising for GDP and employment shares, whose decline for primary production and then manufacturing can be viewed as symptoms of successful economic growth. However, sectoral export shares and indexes of comparative advantage are far more varied across the spectrum of per capita incomes: there are many developing countries with export specialization in services even at low per capita income levels, while export specialization in a few primary products is retained for those high-income countries relatively well-endowed in agricultural land or mineral reserves per worker.

The results clearly indicate that a growing economy may not take a pathway from production and export specialization in primary products to manufactures and then services; some will skip the manufacturing phase, while others will grow rich (and have a large nontradable sector) by remaining specialized in exports of primary products. Chapters 2 and 3 explore what this could mean for the agriculture and tourism sectors of the Lao PDR. As a prelude to that, Box 1.1 debunks the myth that dependence on natural resource–based exports is a curse for developing countries (the "Dutch disease"), and section 1.4 below points to the potential links between the agriculture and tourism sectors.

Box 1.1: Economics of the "Dutch Disease"

The workhorse model of comparative advantage developed in the 19th and 20th centuries suggests that primary product trade will occur between relatively lightly populated economies that are well-endowed with agricultural land and water and/or mineral and energy resources and those that are densely populated with few natural resources per worker. If the stock of natural resources is unchanged, rapid accumulation of produced capital (physical plus human skills and technological knowledge) per unit of available labor will tend to strengthen comparative advantage in non-primary products (Leamer 1987).

By contrast, a new discovery of minerals or energy raw materials would strengthen that country's comparative advantage in mining and weaken its comparative advantage in agricultural and other tradable products as it strengthens the country's real exchange rate. It would also boost national income and hence the demand for nontradables and imported products, which would cause mobile resources to move into the production of nontradable goods and services, further reducing farm and industrial production. Together, those forces reduce the volume of exports from non-booming sectors and the domestic-currency price of those exports, and hence their aggregate value (Corden 1984). Conversely, resource depletion or a fall in the international price of minerals or energy would strengthen the comparative advantage of other sectors producing tradables and weaken the demand for nontradables in a resource-exporting country as its real exchange rate weakens.

A boom in a key export sector could be supply driven (e.g., the discovery of additional mineral deposits or the building of a hydro dam), or demand driven (e.g., a rise in the international price of copper). In the latter case, it will show up as an improvement in the country's international terms of trade and encourage new investment in the mining sector. The more the capital funding for new investment comes in from abroad, the earlier and larger will be the initial appreciation in the real exchange rate. Later, the exchange appreciation will reverse as the boom moves from its investment phase to its export phase and starts to return dividends and possibly capital to foreign investors (Freebairn 2015).

Continued next page

Box 1.1 continued

If the government is uncomfortable with the volatility of the real exchange rate that resource dependence can cause, one option is to establish a sovereign wealth fund such as Norway did. By building it up during a boom (e.g., from expanded mining royalties), there will be less government spending in that part of the cycle; and then it can be drawn down when there is a slump to slow the decline in spending.

Once established, a mining or hydropower export project can be a significant source of government revenue. The use of the windfall by the government will determine how such export-led growth contributes to various groups in society (Menon and Warr 2013). A computable general equilibrium analysis by Warr, Menon, and Yusuf (2012) shows that for the Lao PDR an export-led growth could provide a significant opportunity to reduce national poverty if the windfall is invested in rural areas. See also section 2.3 in the next chapter.

Sources: Corden (1984); Freebairn (2015); Menon and Warr (2013); and Warr, Menon, and Yusuf (2012)

Growth in Agriculture and Tourism: Potential Linkages

As explained in the previous section, growth in any one sector of the economy cannot be understood without referring to what is occurring in (i) markets and policies in other economic sectors, and (ii) the country's international terms of trade and the overseas import barriers faced by its exporters. The discussion also affirms that agriculture remains a viable driver of the economy, and its linkages with other sectors in rural areas need to be strengthened to reduce rural poverty and ensure inclusive growth.

In many countries, tourism is considered an important sector that can have strong forward and backward linkages with agriculture and provide job opportunities in rural areas (Fleischer and Felsenstein 2000). For example, in the PRC, tourism is an important component of its National Strategic Plan for Rural Vitalization, 2018–2022 (Government of the PRC 2018). In 2018, ADB prepared a tourism sector assessment and road map for Cambodia, the Lao PDR, Myanmar, and Viet Nam to support their governments' tourism development plans and strategies and form a joint action program to improve tourism cooperation (ADB 2017b).

A useful framework to depict the relationship of the agriculture sector with other economic sectors, including the tourism sector, and development concepts in general, is the AGRO Matrix that was developed by the ministers of agriculture of the Americas (IICA 2015) (Figure 1.1). The framework is considered to have two pillars: (i) a systemic concept of agriculture and rural life, broken down into three categories or operational areas—rural territories, agricultural value chains, and the national and international context; and (ii) a sustainable development approach consisting of four dimensions or types of actions (production–trade, ecological–environmental, sociocultural–human, and political–institutional) carried out by the stakeholders in each of the three operational areas. Box 1.2 defines the major terms used in the AGRO Matrix.

There are 12 sustainability goals that take into account the spheres of activity covered by the systemic concept and the dimensions of sustainable development: (i) promoting competitive rural enterprises; (ii) integrating chains (or linkages) and strengthening their competitiveness; (iii) promoting an environment conducive to competitive agriculture; (iv) being environmentally responsible in rural areas; (v) from farm to table: promoting integrated environmental management; (vi) participating in building an environmental institutional framework; (vii) quality of life in rural communities: creating know-how and opportunities; (viii) advancing learning and expertise in chains; (ix) promoting policies to create capabilities and opportunities for rural communities; (x) strengthening public and private sector participation and coordinated action between them in territories; (xi) strengthening dialogue and commitments among stakeholders in chains; and (xii) promoting state policies and regional and hemispheric cooperation for agriculture and rural life.

Agritourism can readily be incorporated in the AGRO Matrix. At its most basic level, agritourism is an enterprise that combines elements of agriculture and tourism. Based on the framework shown in the AGRO Matrix, Hepburn (2008) focuses on the forward and backward linkages that take place within this sector. The forward linkages of agritourism are any form of agricultural or rural activity that persuades and encourages tourists to participate and spend their discretionary income on any of the activities offered on site. Backward linkages are the demand for goods and services created by agritourism activities such as food, accommodation, transportation, and personnel like tour guides.

Agritourism, therefore, is a broad concept, which covers a wide range of activities and operations, but essential to all of them is an interaction between agricultural producers, their products, and the tourists. Agritourism applies to

Figure 1.1: The AGRO Matrix

Systematic Concept / Development Approach	Rural Territories	Agricultural Production–Trade Chains	National and International Context	STRATEGIC OBJECTIVES
Production–Trade	I. Promoting competitive rural enterprises	II. Integrating chains and strengthening their competitiveness	III. Promoting an environment conducive to competitive agriculture	Competitiveness
Ecological–Environmental	IV. Being environmentally responsible in the rural areas	V. From farm to table: promoting integrated environmental management	VI. Participating in building an institutional environmental framework	Sustainability
Sociocultural–Human	VII. Quality of life in rural communities: creating know-how and opportunity	VIII. Advancing learning and expertise in the chain	IX. Promoting policies to create capabilities and opportunities for the rural communities	Equity
Political–Institutional	X. Strengthening public and private sector participation and coordinated action between them in the territories	XI. Strengthening dialogue and commitments among actors in the chain	XII. Promoting national policies and regional and hemispheric cooperation for agriculture and rural life	Governance
STRATEGIC OBJECTIVES	Rural Prosperity – Food Security – International Positioning			OVERARCHING GOAL: SUSTAINABLE DEVELOPMENT OF AGRICULTURE AND RURAL MILIEU

Source: IICA (2015).

Box 1.2: Definitions Underlying the AGRO Matrix

The following is a brief description of the spheres of activity in the systemic concept and the dimensions of sustainable development that make up the AGRO Matrix.

Rural territories are geographic areas that have their own history and natural resource base, where agricultural activities are carried out, and the people involved interact with one another and with the natural environment and with other nonagricultural activities and urban centers in the sociocultural, technical–economic, and political–institutional areas.

Production–trade chains are the array of production and distribution processes and interrelationships that link rural and urban areas, and which involve all the economic and social agents engaged in agriculture in a given territory, from the planning of production through to the delivery of products to the national and international end consumers.

The **national and international context** affects the operation of the production–trade chains and the development of territories. It comprises the legal, political, and institutional elements, at the international, national, and local levels, which make up the framework for formulating and implementing public policies, and for effective investment.

The **production–trade dimension** refers to the technical–economic processes that are the foundation of the material progress for facilitating competitiveness; the **ecological–environmental dimension** refers to the (living and nonliving) natural base of production processes which, when combined with human activity, determine its sustainability; the **sociocultural–human dimension** refers to the background, customs, capabilities, rights, needs, and expectations of individual and social groups in terms of equality of opportunities; and the **political–institutional dimension** refers to the international, national, and local institutions, organizations, and networks that affect the governability of society in territories and in political affairs.

Source: IICA (2015).

---

products and services, which combine agriculture—its natural setting and products—with a tourism experience.

Agritourism can be considered a fifth dimension of the sustainable development approach to support achievement of goals aligned to the 12 mentioned earlier. At the very least, agritourism plays a role in three of the four dimensions: production–trade, ecological–environmental, and sociocultural–human. Policy makers can add to the sustainability goals by specifying how agritourism interacts with rural territories, agricultural value chains, and the national and international context as shown in the example of Table 1.4.

Table 1.4: Agritourism and Its Multidimensions

	Rural Territories	Agricultural Production–Trade Chains	National and International Context
Agritourism	Promote tourist visits to rural areas	Develop food tourism	Encourage regional cooperation in tourism

Source: Authors' application of the AGRO Matrix.

Agritourism can increase agricultural production in the Lao PDR, by encouraging new participants in the industry, while exposing visitors to local products. Backward linkages are strengthened by providing more sources of demand for agriculture and rural-based goods and services. A recently conducted survey in the Lao PDR, for example, found that the craft sector provided the largest employment opportunities among tourism-related enterprises, followed by transport and accommodation enterprises (Ministry of Education and Sports 2018).

Forward linkages are strengthened by attracting more visitors to the rural areas and enhancing the reputation of the Lao PDR. In the international context, agritourism encourages regional cooperation among neighboring countries. An example is the Visit ASEAN program.

While not mentioned explicitly, inclusive growth plays an important role in this framework. First, since agritourism deals mainly with the rural sector, the largest concentration of poverty is targeted. Second, inclusivity is a necessary condition for sustainability. Society cannot survive indefinitely if inequities are large and persistent. Conflicts will arise and tear at the social fabric. Last, the matrix indicates that one of the four condensed characteristics of the 12 objectives is equity. In other words, these objectives are designed to promote inclusivity.

One area that should be emphasized is food tourism (e.g., Slocum and Curtis 2018). Rather than importing food from outside a destination, businesses promote local food and increase the interrelationship between local agriculture and tourism. Food tourism offers two unique advantages for a region:

(i) it provides a new experience for tourists and encourages increased visitation; and (ii) it enhances economic impacts—such as higher farm income and job creation—to the community where tourists visit. Food tourism has the potential to increase economic multipliers, decrease leakages to a destination, and diversify rural areas with a strong agricultural economic base.

Table 1.5 provides a quantitative measure of the linkage between food and tourism in the Lao PDR. Data are obtained from input–output tables in various years. The food component is proxied by the agriculture sector in the input–output table, while tourism is represented by the hotel and restaurant sector. In 2010, total output in the agriculture sector was $2,155 million. Only $8 million or 0.4% flowed into the hotel and restaurant sector. While there was a sharp increase in 2010–2013, the available data show a stagnant relationship in 2013–2017. Clearly, there is room for the relationship between the two sectors to expand, and one channel is through promoting agritourism.

Table 1.5: Components of the Agriculture Sector in the Lao PDR Input–Output Table

Year	Hotel and Restaurant Sector ($ million)	Total Output ($ million)	Share of H&R to Total Output (%)
2010	8	2,115	0.4
2013	51	2,383	2.1
2015	56	2,664	2.1
2017	50	3,038	1.6

H&R = hotel and restaurant, Lao PDR = Lao People's Democratic Republic.
Source: ADB Data Library. Lao People's Democratic Republic: Input–Output Economic Indicators. https://data.adb.org/dataset/lao-pdr-input-output-economic-indicators (accessed 25 November 2020).

The 12 objectives—or 15 if agritourism is included as the fifth dimension—can be translated into specific policies. For example, particularly important in an emerging agrarian economy are changes in infrastructure. The development of major rail and road networks can hugely reduce trade costs, particularly for those close to these networks. New electricity and communication towers usually accompany transport infrastructure, further reducing the costs of doing business along the route. Feeder roads, electricity, and communication services can be built to reach more-distant rural areas, allowing farmers to sell their products beyond their local market and at higher farm-gate prices, and expand the opportunities for underemployed farm family members to commute to off-farm part-time jobs. The higher farm incomes could, on the other hand, encourage younger family members to remain and help in farming, raising the productivity of labor on farms due to the lower average age of farm workers.

As potential tourism venues are located in currently hard-to-reach rural areas, investments in rail and road investments (or a new airport) can create job opportunities in the services sector. The production and sale of handicrafts and farm outputs also increase direct income when tourism expands in the rural areas, as described in a recent report (Ministry of Education and Sports 2018). However, if growth in tourism is confined to the small number of large cities in the country, mobile resources will tend to be drawn away from farms in the same way other urban developments have done.

The COVID-19 Pandemic and Its Impact on Agriculture and Tourism Sectors

The Lao PDR reported its first two COVID-19 cases on 24 March 2020. A nationwide lockdown followed on 30 March 2020, prohibiting residents from leaving their homes except for essentials. All international ports of entry were closed to tourists, issuance of tourist visas suspended, and interprovincial travel banned. The quick action of the government prevented a significant rise in cases in 2020. In May 2020, ADB approved a $20 million COVID-19 emergency loan under the Greater Mekong Subregion Health Security Project to support the Ministry of Health in procuring protective equipment, laboratory equipment, testing kits, medical devices, and ambulances. Supplies and training to frontline health workers on infection prevention and control, lab testing, and clinical care for COVID-19 patients were also provided (ADB 2020b).

In 31 March 2021, the Lao PDR reported only 49 confirmed COVID-19 cases and no deaths. However, in April 2021 the country witnessed a new outbreak of COVID-19, with cases rising to 2,356, with three deaths by 7 July 2021.[6] To respond to the rise in cases, the Lao PDR government imposed preventive measures including lockdowns and domestic travel restrictions. However, on 4 May 2020, the nationwide lockdown and intraprovincial travel restrictions were lifted. By 18 May 2020 tourist sites were opened and interprovincial travel was again permitted, including domestic flights (Savankham 2020b).

---

[6]   Government of the Lao PDR. Ministry of Health. COVID-19 Dashboard (in Lao). https://www.covid19.gov.la/index.php.

Although the country has thus far avoided severe health impacts from the COVID-19 pandemic, the economy has suffered. The pandemic had a devastating impact on tourism as international arrivals to the country dropped by 81.5% in 2020.

The agriculture sector was not spared either. In April 2020, the World Food Programme (WFP) in collaboration with the Food and Agriculture Organization of the United Nations (FAO) and the Ministry of Agriculture and Forestry, performed a survey to assess the impact of the pandemic on food security and agriculture.[7] Survey results showed a significant reduction of agricultural activities in many provinces in the Lao PDR, specifically in Louang-Namtha, Xaisomboun, and Savannakhet. Interestingly, Attapu experienced more than 40% increase in agricultural activities while also reporting some reduction (Figure 1.2).

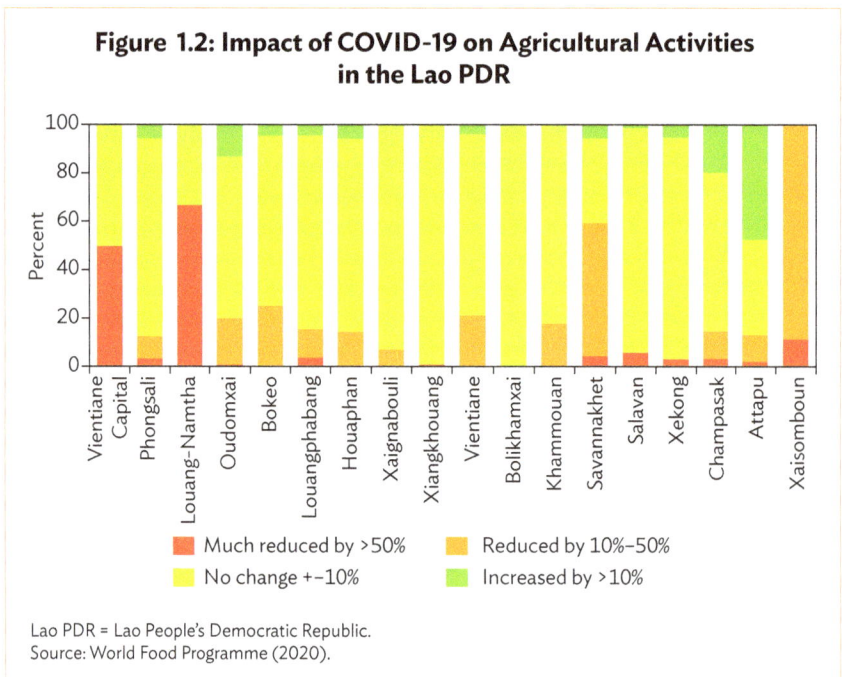

Figure 1.2: Impact of COVID-19 on Agricultural Activities in the Lao PDR

Legend:
- Much reduced by >50%
- Reduced by 10%–50%
- No change +–10%
- Increased by >10%

Lao PDR = Lao People's Democratic Republic.
Source: World Food Programme (2020).

---

[7]   The survey was conducted in Vientiane Capital and 17 provinces in the Lao PDR and completed a total of 1,007 interviews by phone from 21 April to 30 April 2020, within the period of the full lockdown. While there are limitations to this study including small sample sizes in some provinces, the study sought to capture the perceptions of local "experts" and obtain an informed understanding of the situation.

The pandemic also affected the income and sales of farmers. According to the survey, 32% of farmers indicated that they could not sell their produce at the pre-COVID-19 price level. As a result, agricultural sales declined by 22% and prices decreased by 15%, and all provinces reported their farm incomes either declining or remaining steady. The Savannakhet district reported the greatest loss in farm income (Figure 1.3).

Figure 1.3: Impact of COVID-19 on Farm Income

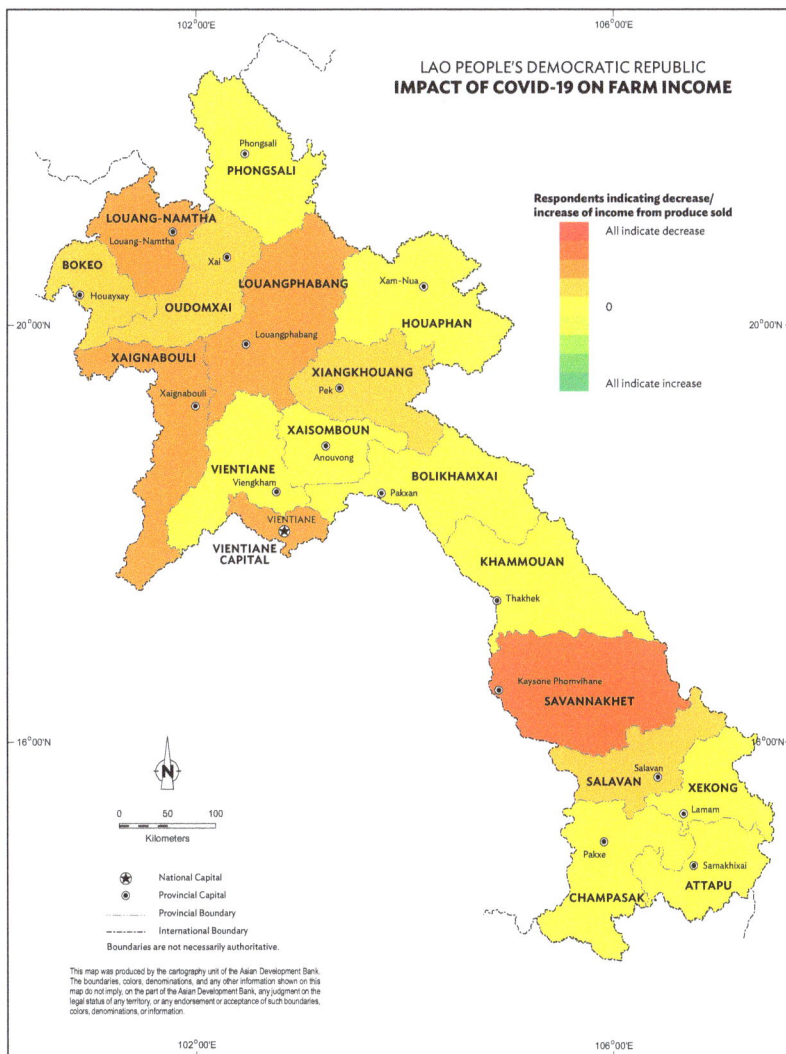

Source: World Food Programme (2020).

According to Namvong (2020), Lao farmers who produce highly perishable seasonal products, like fruits and vegetables, have been the most affected. The closure of restaurants and the shutdown of the tourism industry largely contributed to the reduction of demand for agricultural products. The Lao Farmer Network reported cases of farmers feeding cabbages to livestock or leaving the produce in the fields to rot. However, some commercial crops such as maize and cassava were relatively unaffected, since these were not planted or harvested during the lockdown. Others, such as coffee and tea, were less affected because of their longer storage period.

The joint FAO–WFP assessment study identified several recommendations to mitigate the impacts of COVID-19 in the sector: (i) reduce restrictions on traders and middlemen to improve access to food and alleviate issues of increased food prices and availability; (ii) provide support to vulnerable households with insufficient access to food through in-kind or cash support (for example, cash or food assistance for assets) to build longer-term resilience to food insecurity; (iii) provide supplements to seasonal agriculture, particularly at the household level, through home gardens, small livestock raising, and fish culture; and (iv) improve nutritional awareness within the country.

While the Government of the Lao PDR is taking all necessary measures to address the pandemic with support from various development agencies, FAO and the WFP are cooperating with the Lao Ministry of Agriculture and Forestry to draft a response plan. The ministry has also provided direct assistance, such as seed supply, home gardening kits, animal health-care items, and technical support to help communities continue to produce local food and increase self-sufficiency amid the pandemic.

Overview of the Report

The rest of the report expands on the topics of agriculture and tourism and the synergy between the two sectors. Chapter 2 gives a detailed discussion on how the farm sector can contribute more to economic development in the Lao PDR. The main issue is enhancing agricultural productivity and at the same time distributing the benefits more equitably. While there have been significant achievements, more work needs to be done. For example, public and private resources have to be channeled to bring modern technology to rural areas to spur innovation in agricultural production and processing and harness digital technology to expand market access, thus increasing farm productivity and raising rural incomes.

Chapter 3 analyzes the potential of tourism in the Lao PDR. Despite the global tourism downturn in 2020, the Lao PDR has several strengths that can help its tourism industry quickly recover once international borders reopen to tourists. These include its strategic location in the center of populous Southeast Asia, with nearby markets showing a strong and growing affinity for the types of culture and nature-based tourism that the country offers. While organic food production, agro-food tourism industries, handicrafts, and agro-processing of local food products have emerged as employment and income sources, these will need to be supported to bring better opportunities for local producers and farmers, and thus achieve more inclusive growth.

The results of the ADB surveys of tourism enterprise in 2019 and 2020 in four major tourism destinations in the Lao PDR are described in Chapter 4. Findings show that the tourism sector has strong linkages to the domestic labor market and the agriculture sector, which means that the locals are benefiting from the expansion of tourism services.

Analysis in the first four chapters clearly shows that harnessing the potential of tourism services provides an opportunity for the Lao PDR to create good jobs, especially in rural areas and among women and other disadvantaged groups. Unfortunately, tourism is one of the worst affected sectors by the ongoing COVID-19 pandemic. The 2020 survey shows that the majority of tourism enterprises will be unable to endure the protracted COVID-19 crisis, without financial assistance. Chapter 5 looks into both short- and medium-term measures to respond to the pandemic and the opportunities that will emerge after it has subsided. The priority would be to control the spread of the virus to protect public health by implementing well-designed travel bans and restrictions and implement the rollout of vaccines so as to achieve herd immunity from COVID-19.[8] However, international tourism will become even more competitive once the pandemic subsides and international borders start to reopen. It is critical that the Lao PDR continues to invest in tourism infrastructure and services so that it is able to attract high-spending tourists. More importantly, to fully benefit from the expansion of tourism services, linkages between tourism and other sectors, particularly agriculture, should be strengthened. Investments in rural infrastructure, research and development, and extension services are crucial to modernize the agriculture sector and achieve more inclusive growth.

---

[8] According to the National Taskforce Committee for COVID-19 Prevention and Control, about 1.6 million people, or 20% of the Lao population, are expected to be vaccinated in 2021, and the vaccination coverage is expected to rise to 50% in 2022 (Vientiane Times 2021c).

CHAPTER 2

Agriculture's Contribution to Inclusive Growth in the Lao PDR

Kym Anderson, Takashi Yamano, and Jindra Samson

Agriculture is central to the Lao PDR economy; it is one of the most important sectors to foster inclusive growth. Development in the sector over the last 3 decades has played a key role in reducing poverty in the entire country, particularly in many parts of remote regions that rely on agriculture for livelihood and subsistence. In 2018–2020, an annual average share of 66% of the country's total workforce was employed in agriculture—one of the highest in Asia. The majority of rural household income in the Lao PDR comes from crop production and sales of livestock and forest products. Food, particularly rice, accounts for about 50% of the general household consumption, and about 60% share of the low-income households (ADB 2017a). This makes low-income households highly vulnerable to food price shocks.

With much to offer, Lao agriculture has great potential for growth. Policies and interventions should focus on increasing agricultural productivity by improving agricultural systems and value chains that can offer a more secure food supply, livelihood, and higher income for its rural population. The Lao PDR will need to harmonize integrative programs to strengthen linkages among sectors—like agriculture, manufacturing, tourism, and services that will position the country in the global market—as these will help advance local industries to where the country has the highest comparative advantage. It will need to support emerging niche markets—such as organic food products, agro-food tourism industries, handicrafts, and agro-processing of local food products—to bring better opportunities for local producers and farmers, thus achieving more inclusive growth.

This chapter begins with an overview of agricultural development in the Lao PDR. Section 2.1 summarizes the role of agriculture and why it is the most important sector to foster inclusive growth. Section 2.2 looks at the development of relevant agricultural policies and strategies that have shaped and advanced the sector. Section 2.3 describes the country's agricultural and farmland holding systems. Section 2.4 discusses the stature, challenges, and achievements in agricultural production. Section 2.5 describes agricultural markets and trade from the 1990s to the present, and section 2.6 presents the increasing intersectoral linkages between agriculture and tourism. The final section recommends policy options for inclusive growth in the agriculture sector.

Agriculture as a Driver of Inclusive Growth

The agriculture and natural resource sectors remain central to the Lao PDR's steadfast economic growth. Development in the agriculture sector has been crucial in achieving poverty reduction in many parts of the country. The Lao economy, like other economies in Southeast Asia, has undergone structural transformation from a primarily agrarian economy to a more diversified and market-oriented one. Table 2.1 shows that agriculture's annual average gross domestic product (GDP) share fell from 20% in 2012 to 16% in 2019, while the share of the industry sector increased from 36% in 2012 to 40% in 2019. Between these periods, the agriculture sector grew by only about 3%, with growth largely coming from the crop and livestock (4%) and fishery (5%) sectors. Growth contraction was largely in the forestry sector.

Table 2.1: Changes in the Sector Composition of GDP
(%)

Sector	Subsector	GDP Share (2012)	GDP Share (2019)	Average Annual Growth (2012–2019)
Agriculture		**20.4**	**15.5**	**2.6**
	(a) Crops, livestock, and hunting	15.3	12.2	2.8
	(b) Forestry	2.4	1.0	(5.6)
	(c) Fishing	2.7	2.4	3.8
Industry		**35.6**	**39.8**	**7.3**
	(a) Mining and quarrying	12.6	8.4	0.1
	(b) Manufacturing	9.9	9.1	4.9
	(c) Electricity and water	7.1	12.1	12.6
	(d) Construction	5.7	10.2	14.3
Services		**44.1**	**44.7**	**5.5**

( ) = negative, GDP = gross domestic product.
Sources: Official Lao data through UNData. http://data.un.org/Explorer.aspx?d=SNA; Lao Statistical Information Service. Lao Statistics Bureau. https://laosis.lsb.gov.la/tblInfo/TblInfoList.do (accessed 11 January 2021).

Food crops and livestock production have grown at the same fast pace, but nonfood agricultural production has soared more quickly. The take-off in annual outputs of nonfood agricultural products was relatively slow during the 2 decades prior to 2005, but it has accelerated since then (Figure 2.1). Overall agricultural output grew by 6.3% per year from 1991 to 2010, and by 5.7% from 2010 to 2019.

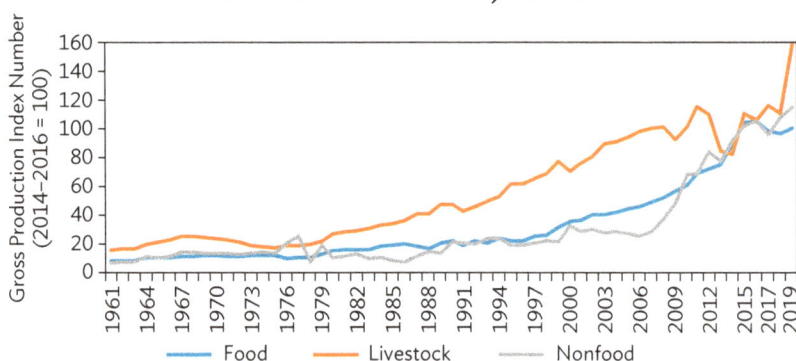

Figure 2.1: Indexes for Food Crops, Livestock, and Nonfood Crop Production in the Lao PDR, 1961–2019

Lao PDR = Lao People's Democratic Republic.
Source: Food and Agriculture Organization of the United Nations. FAOSTAT. http://www.fao.org/faostat/en/#home (accessed 11 January 2021).

Agriculture as the Largest Source of Employment and Rural Household Income

The share of agricultural employment in total Lao PDR workforce declined from 80% in 2000 to 60% in 2020, but it is still among the highest in Asia (Figure 2.2). Based on the Lao Agriculture Census (2011), about 66% of rural household income in the Lao PDR comes from agriculture and primarily earned from crop production and sales of livestock and forest products (Ministry of Agriculture and Forestry 2014).

The income shares, however, vary among provinces (Figure 2.3). The crop income share is highest in the northern provinces of Xaignabouli (78%), followed by Houaphan (72%), Louang-Namtha (67%), and Oudomxai (66%). In central and southern provinces, income sources are more diverse. In some provinces closer to the capital city and bordering neighboring countries, the share of income from nonagriculture sectors is relatively high—for example it is 53.6% in Attapu, 50.7% in Vientiane Capital, 48.6% in Savannakhet, and 47.8% in Khammouan.

Figure 2.2: Structure of Employment in the Lao PDR and Selected Countries, 2000, 2010, and 2020
(% of total employment)

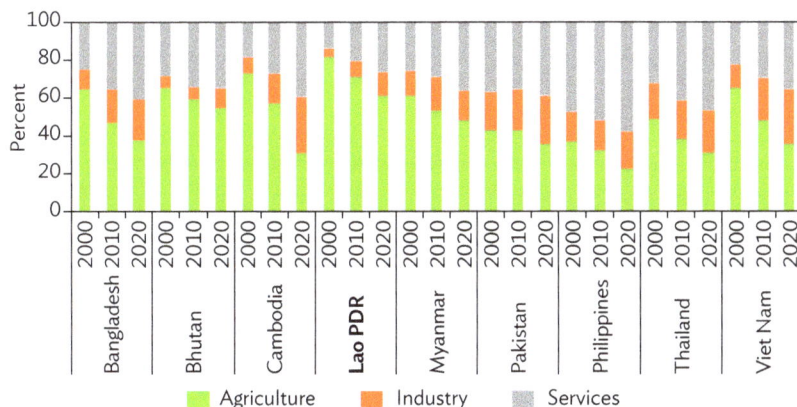

Lao PDR = Lao People's Democratic Republic.
Source: ILOSTAT. https://ilostat.ilo.org/data/ (accessed 11 January 2021).

Figure 2.3: Sources of Household Income by Province in the Lao PDR, 2011

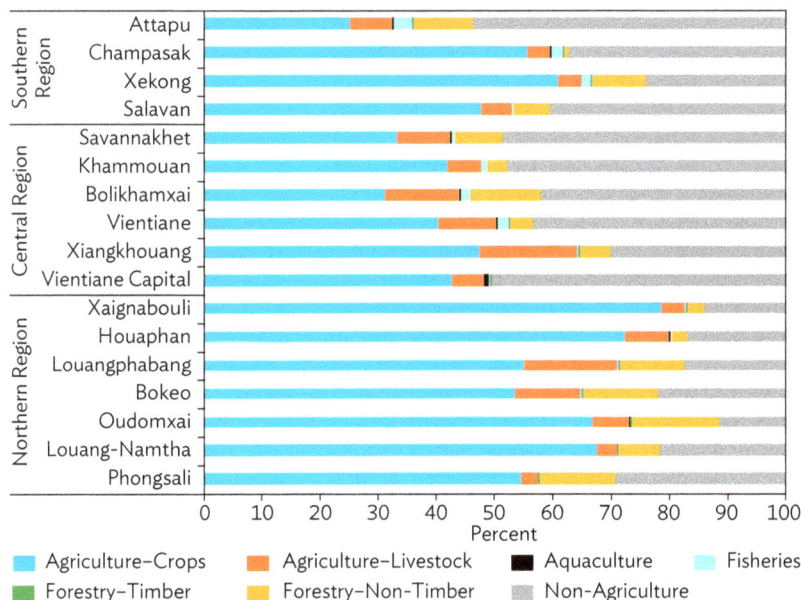

Lao PDR = Lao People's Democratic Republic.
Source: Ministry of Agriculture and Forestry (2014).

In some provinces that have become better connected by road to Vientiane Capital and other urban centers, farm households have gained access to more economic opportunities and job markets, improving their income sources from off-farm employment such as casual or regular part-time employment, government salaries, and remittances from family members. Opportunities for farm workers in the south and center exist abroad in Thailand, in the PRC for those in the north, and in Viet Nam for those in the eastern border.

Even so, much scope remains for strengthening links to urban and regional markets, especially for the rural regions that have benefited least from the recent economic growth. The income inequality identified by Warr, Rasphone, and Menon (2018) is evident not only between urban and rural groups but also within the rural population. Pockets of poverty still exist in the upland areas and among rural ethnic minority groups and rural subsistence farmers. Economic growth to date has benefited people in the lowlands more than those in the upland where ethnic minority groups are concentrated.

There is also inequality of opportunity within the rural areas. Women make up a little over half of the agricultural rural workforce (FAO 2018) and work several more hours per week than men, but they have less access to credit and the latest technologies. This is especially true in upland ethnic minority areas. Women who do have access to land more often engage in commercial production to supplement household income. This suggests that providing more opportunities to women in the rural areas could contribute to inclusive economic growth.

Gateway Out of Poverty and Malnutrition

Poverty is greatest among people who are dependent primarily on agriculture for livelihood and employment (Figure 2.4). While rice production has increased fourfold since the mid-1980s, undernourishment remains a serious concern, especially in the upland and northern rural areas. The Lao PDR still ranks 87th out of 117 countries on the Global Hunger Index (IFPRI 2019). The incidence of malnourishment is closely correlated with poverty, but also because high transport costs prevent rural residents from gaining access to a micronutrient-rich diversified diet beyond the locally produced fresh fruits and vegetables and protein from fish and livestock. Even crop–livestock mixed farms do not bring enough diversity to farm household diets to lower indicators of malnourishment such as stunting, wasting, and child mortality (Parvathi 2018).

Figure 2.4: Poverty Headcount Rate by Main Employment Status of Household Head in the Lao PDR, 2002-2003 to 2018-2019
(%)

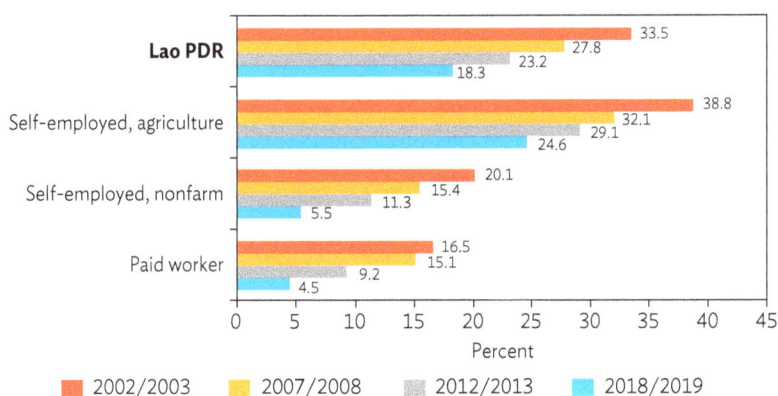

Lao PDR = Lao People's Democratic Republic.
Notes: Nominal official poverty lines (per person per month) used for each year are (i) 2002/2003: KN92,959.6; (ii) 2007/2008: KN159,611.9; (iii) 2012/2013: KN203,613.6; and (iv) 2018/2019: KN280,910.
Sources: Lao Statistics Bureau (2014); and Lao Statistics Bureau and the World Bank (2020).

The country's rich natural land and water resource endowments should enable the Lao PDR's agriculture sector to achieve its maximum production potential, provide food security for its people, and create rural livelihood. With the right strategies and policies, broad-based agricultural growth can help boost the purchasing power of the poor, enhance incomes, and reduce the unit cost of most household expenditures (ADB 2017a).

Relevant Agricultural Policies and Strategies that Shaped the Sector

After the introduction of the open-door policy under the New Economic Mechanism (NEM), the Lao PDR's socioeconomic development shifted from its natural (self-sufficient) economy to a more market-oriented one, placing great importance to agriculture and forestry as the basis for industrialization. As more investments were poured on agricultural infrastructure—such as irrigation systems, reservoirs, and water stations that were built all over the country—agricultural development expanded, enabling farmers to enjoy two-season cropping and to diversify crops. Agricultural practices have gradually shifted from those that had put a high toll on its natural resources (such as slash and burn, shifting cultivation) to improved and modern methods. Technical-scientific infrastructure such as research and experiment centers as well as technical service stations have been built and developed. These have opened the gateway for agricultural production to expand and for the Lao PDR to become more self-sufficient in food.

In 1991, as the Lao PDR adopted a new Constitution, the Fifth Plenary Meeting of the Party Central Committee reiterated the basic objective of its agricultural policy: a shift from subsistence production to cash crop production via crop diversification and improved linkages to export markets. Thus, agricultural policy evolved to commodity production. Subsequent five-year plans (1996–2000 and 2001–2005) articulated the same. In the fifth National Socioeconomic Development Plan (NSEDP), special emphasis was given to reducing slash-and-burn agriculture and poppy production.

In the sixth NSEDP (2006–2010), the agriculture sector pushed for commercialization with a view to increase agricultural products for export. The plan identified among its main strategies (i) tackling food security for the 47 poorest districts; (ii) diversifying crops by developing agricultural areas to specialize in Lao-specific plantation crops, vegetables, and fruits; (iii) building irrigation facilities in agricultural production areas, establishing market-oriented agriculture by developing an appropriate framework for credit mechanisms, product distribution, technical infrastructure, price adjustments, and opening up opportunities for export markets; (iv) managing land use for agricultural production including allowing the lease of land to foreigners for large-scale agricultural projects; and (v) mitigating the effects of climate change.

The seventh NSEDP was touted successful in gradually weaning the country from agriculture and in increasing the shares of services and industry in the national economy. Overall, production of agricultural products increased although much of these were still raw materials, lacking value-added processing.

The eighth NSEDP (2016–2020) emphasized the development of the agriculture and forestry sectors to ensure sustainable production of food and commercial goods. It focused on the application of new technology to improve processing of products, such as international standard rice mills and furniture factories for wood products, to increase value added. Land zoning to allocate land for particular crops, land registration to discourage conversion of irrigated rice fields, and issuance of agricultural land titles to farmer families are some of its defined strategies.

The most recent Agricultural development Strategy to the year 2025 and Vision to the year 2030 (ADS 2025) seeks to ensure national food security through sustainable agriculture that contributes to national economic growth, industrialization, and modernization. The overall targets of the ADS 2025 are to (i) increase agricultural production, (ii) improve and enhance agriculture competitiveness in terms of quality, through (iii) enforcing standards and regulations, and (iv) guaranteeing food security and safety through compliance with basic sanitary and phytosanitary standards. Agricultural production will play an essential role in (i) creating jobs, (ii) generating livelihood and income that will in turn (iii) reduce disparities between urban and rural areas, and (iv) integrate rural development. Box 2.1 shows the overall defined goals and program goals of this strategy. The ADS is largely consistent with the AGRO Matrix framework presented in Chapter 1.

Box 2.1: Agricultural Development Strategy to the Year 2025 and Vision to the Year 2030

Overall Goals:

1.   Economy has strongly grown in line with industrialization and modernization direction, comprehensive infrastructure, ensuring economic growth at a constant level; effective, stable, and assured food security which strongly ensures quality in terms of nutrition; and producing agricultural products with quantity and quality that are highly competitive as well as adaptable to climate change.

2.   Agricultural production is in line with sanitary principles, clean, safe for producers' and consumers' health, and environmentally friendly.

3.   Agricultural production has made contribution in many aspects such as creation of employment, income generation for people, reduction of gap between cities and rural areas, construction of new rural areas alongside the protection of symbolic cultures of all ethnic people, environmental protection, and stability and balance of the ecological system.

Program Goal 1: Food Production – to ensure nutrition of people to provide energy of at least 2,600 kilocalories per person per day, which includes rice and starch covering approximately 62%; meat, eggs, and fish approximately 10%; vegetables, fruits, and beans approximately 6%; and fat, sugar, and milk approximately 22%.

Program Goal 2: Agricultural Commodity Production – to make the production of agricultural commodities grow to create the basic factors for industrialization and modernization, ensuring both quantity and quality and aiming to access domestic, regional, and international markets in connection with the improvement of farmers' groups and producers' and agriculture processing associations by making effort toward agricultural production of main goods.

Source: Ministry of Agriculture and Forestry (2015b).

Agricultural Systems and Land Farmholdings

The Lao PDR has an estimated total agricultural area of about 2.4 million hectares (ha) (Table 2.2), of which only about 59% (1.4 million ha) is classified arable, only 4.2% is planted with permanent crops, while some 37% is used for pasture and meadows. The low ratio of cultivated to total land area is partly due to constraints brought by its natural topography, a substantial level of water-logged areas, and the presence of many unexploded ordnance scattered throughout 15 of its 17 provinces. The Lao PDR's agricultural land area makes up about only 10% of the total land area, one of the smallest shares among Southeast Asian countries.

The Lao PDR climate is tropical, with rainy season from May to October and dry season from November to April. Monsoon rains bring an annual average precipitation rate of about 1,600 millimeters, more or less evenly distributed across its provinces.[9] The country is rich in water resources—it has far more freshwater per hectare of arable land compared with other countries in the region. Its forests cover about 68% of total land area, serving as habitat to a wide diversity of species and cradling the country's rich mineral resources.

Table 2.2: Major Categories of Land Use in the Lao PDR and Neighboring Countries, 2018

	Country	Total Land Area (million ha)	Total Agricultural Land (million ha)	Land Area (% share)		Agricultural Area (% share)		
				Agriculture	Forests	Arable Land	Permanent Crops	Pastures/ Meadows
1	Cambodia	17.7	5.7	32.0	56.5	70.7	2.7	26.5
2	**Lao PDR**	**23.1**	**2.4**	**10.3**	**67.9**	**58.9**	**4.2**	**36.9**
3	Myanmar	65.3	12.6	19.2	48.2	85.9	11.7	2.5
4	Thailand	51.1	21.1	41.2	37.2	74.8	21.4	3.8
5	Viet Nam	31.0	10.8	35.0	45.0	60.0	34.1	5.9

ha = hectare, Lao PDR = Lao People's Democratic Republic.
Source: Food and Agriculture Organization of the United Nations. FAOSTAT. Food and Agriculture Data. http://www.fao.org/faostat/en/#home (accessed January 2021).

---

[9]   Ministry of Natural Resources and Environment. Department of Meteorology and Hydrology. http://www.monre.gov.la/home/index.php.

According to the Lao Census of Agriculture 2010/2011 (Ministry of Agriculture and Forestry 2014), the distribution of farmholdings varies greatly across regions but is dominated by smallholders operating on less than 3 hectares of land. At the national level, 22% of farm households operate on less than a hectare, 31% on about 1–2 ha, and 19% on about 2–3 ha. Farm households with landholdings of 3 ha or more comprise 27% of total households but occupy 58% of the country's total farmland (Table 2.3).

Table 2.3: Provincial Distribution of Landholdings by Farm Size, 2011

Province	Distributed Number of Landholdings (%)				No. of Farm Households ('000)
	< 1 ha	1–2 ha	2–3 ha	> 3 ha	
Northern Region					
Phongsali	32.9	37.6	17.7	11.8	28.4
Louang-Namtha	15.9	36.8	26.6	20.6	26.2
Oudomxai	16.0	34.3	24.0	25.4	44.6
Bokeo	19.8	38.7	21.6	19.6	24.8
Louangphabang	11.3	25.8	20.9	41.5	59.5
Houaphan	41.8	39.6	12.4	5.8	42.3
Xaignabouli	18.7	26.5	18.6	35.1	63.1
Central Region					
Vientiane Capital	42.8	22.0	9.8	20.6	42.8
Xiangkhouang	27.3	35.8	17.4	19.5	36.2
Vientiane	26.9	26.5	16.8	29.6	62.7
Bolikhamxai	21.3	34	19.9	23.4	35.0
Khammouan	25.0	29.8	19.5	25.0	51.2
Savannakhet	15.6	27.6	19.8	36.8	108.6
Southern Region					
Salavan	15.4	31.5	21.4	31.5	50.1
Xekong	21.2	36.7	15.8	25.0	12.9
Champasak	18.1	36.2	21.7	22.3	75.4
Attapu	18.4	40.0	22.7	18.0	19.1
Total	**21.9**	**31.4**	**19.2**	**26.7**	**782.8**

Region	Distribution of Landholding Area (%)				Total Area ('000)
	< 1 ha	1–2 ha	2–3 ha	> 3 ha	
Northern region	5.7	20.1	20.7	53.6	650
Central region	5.3	15.0	16.1	63.7	864
Southern region	4.3	21.0	21.7	53.1	356
Total	**5.2**	**17.9**	**18.7**	**58.2**	**1,870**

ha = hectare.
Source: Ministry of Agriculture and Forestry (2014).

In the central provinces, the largest proportions of farm households with less than 1 ha are located in Vientiane Capital (43%), followed by Houaphan (42%), Phongsali (33%), and Vientiane Province (27%). A large share of the total area in these provinces is planted with rain-fed and irrigated rice crops, while shifting cultivation is practiced in upland agriculture. The largest proportions of farm households with 3 ha and over are found in Louangphabang (41%), Savannakhet (37%), Xaignabouli (35%), and Salavan (31%).

The agricultural systems in the Lao PDR are unique for each region, differing in terms of conditions and production potential. It can be classified broadly into four major systems: lowland, upland, plateau, and mixed systems (Figure 2.5). According to the Lao Census of Agriculture 2010/2011 (Ministry of Agriculture and Forestry 2014), 51% of the country's farm area is in the lowland areas, 25% lies in the uplands, 23% is found along plateaus, and the rest in what is classified as mixed systems (Figure 2.6). Among the provinces, Savannakhet, Louangphabang, Vientiane, and Champasak have the largest productive agricultural land areas in the country.

Farming in the lowlands is predominantly based on rain-fed and irrigated rice systems, with integrated mixed-crop systems of vegetables, groundnuts, and fruit trees. Many smallholder farm households follow a mixed farming system, particularly in the uplands of the northern provinces where the practice of shifting cultivation is most prominent. In the rain-fed paddy fields of the central and southern provinces, crops are more diversified, with farmers growing vegetables, groundnuts, starchy crops, and tropical fruits. Recently, cultivation in many parts of the country has expanded to commercial crops such as rubber, sugarcane, cassava, and maize.

Contract farming and concessions have benefited from recent foreign investments, particularly on commercial crops like rubber, sugar, maize, and coffee. Foreign direct investment (FDI) in agriculture was restricted in the country until 2005 but has expanded rapidly since. A study by Baumüller and Lazarus (2012) notes that agricultural FDI in the northern region is focused more on contract farming arrangements, while in the south and central plains FDI is targeted on large land concessions. This is understandable because the plains are better suited for large-scale agriculture and have superior links to markets and processors. The major commercial crops are rubber, sugar, maize, and coffee. Companies from the PRC invest in rubber production in the northern uplands via contract farming, while Viet Nam companies in the south typically use land concessions. Chinese and Thai investors focus on sugar production through concessions and contract farming, while Thai investors, particularly in border provinces, concentrate on maize production.

Figure 2.5: Lao PDR Agricultural Systems by Elevation

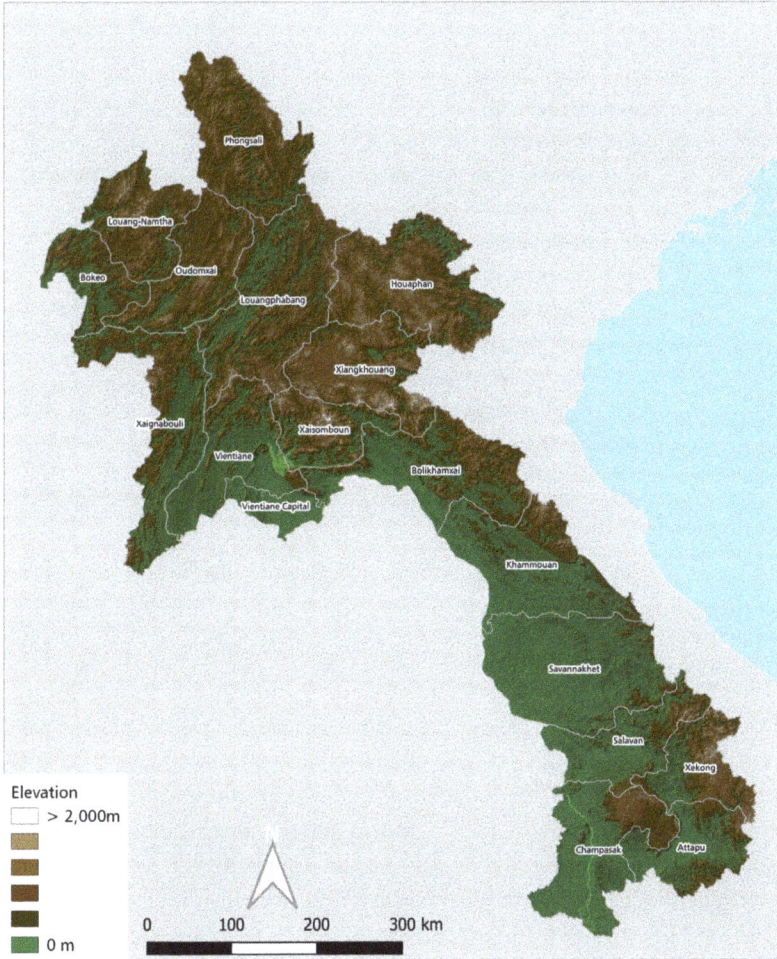

km = kilometer, Lao PDR = Lao People's Democratic Republic, m = meter.
Notes: This map combines two data sets (land cover and elevation) to depict a realistic overview of the Lao PDR terrain. Land cover refers to the physical appearance of the earth's surface, e.g., vegetation, water, or bare soil. The European Space Agency (ESA) has been continuously monitoring and classifying global land cover since 1992. In October 2019, ESA released the latest update on the earth's land surface including the 2018 land cover featured in this map.
Source: 30-Meter Resolution Elevation Data from the Shuttle Radar Topography Mission. https://dwtkns.com/srtm30m/ (accessed 2020).

Figure 2.6: Lao PDR Agricultural Topology by Area and Province, 2011

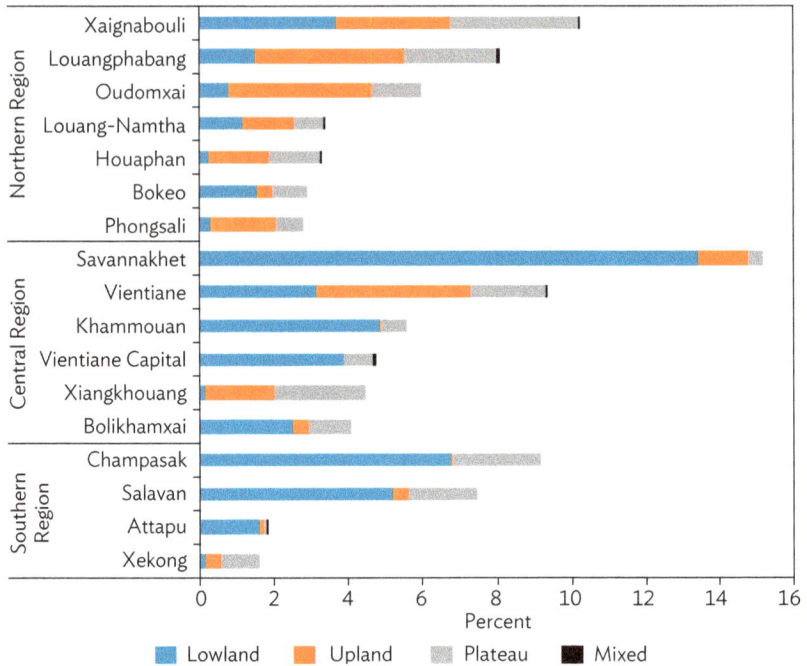

Lao PDR = Lao People's Democratic Republic.
Source: Ministry of Agriculture and Forestry (2014).

Although contract growing and crop concessions have contributed to the growth of agricultural productivity at the macroeconomic level, their effects are not as positive at the local level, especially for smallholder farmers. A study by Annim and Gaiha (2012) found that FDI in agriculture had a minor negative impact on the value of crops and a minor positive impact on the value of livestock and fisheries. Increased production of cash crops can come at the cost of food security as farmers have either switched to producing cash crops or resettled away from their farming lands.

The lack of cohesive smallholder farmer organizations puts them at a disadvantage in contract farming arrangements, as they may be reduced to "plantation labor." Farmers could have higher cash incomes, but also incur higher levels of indebtedness, face worsening environmental conditions with increased use of chemicals, and may be confronted with the loss of a more resilient and diversified farming system. Note too, that the Lao PDR has one of the longest concession periods in Southeast Asia, with some leases stretching to 70 years (Schoenweger and Ullenberg 2010).

Stature, Achievements, and Key Challenges in Agricultural Production in the Lao PDR

To consolidate the economic achievements of the Lao PDR, particularly in the agriculture sector, policy reforms have to be instituted and programs implemented to overcome specific challenges but with the overall goal of enhancing productivity. The policies and programs can be guided by both the ADS discussed in Box 2.1 and the AGRO Matrix presented in Chapter 1.

Following the operational areas in the AGRO Matrix framework, it is important to analyze the value chain of essential commodities (such as rice, for example, as discussed in Box 2.2). Bottlenecks in the value chains can be identified and appropriate measures to address the constraints prescribed. The national and regional milieu is another important component of the framework.

Section 2.5 expounds on the link between agriculture and tourism and the issues at the core of strengthening that link. As explained in Chapter 1, the links between the two sectors can be defined in terms of backward and forward linkages; and several examples are analyzed in section 2.5. An important dimension of agritourism is anchored on the operational area of rural territories (Box 2.4 on the Nam Ha Ecotourism Project and Box 2.5 on the Phutawen Farm are useful examples).

Agricultural production has been moving away from subsistence farming to market-oriented and diversified production in the last 3 decades. In 2018, the country's total agricultural production value was estimated at $6.1 billion, largely from vegetables (21%), rice (20%), and livestock (20%) production (Figure 2.7). Cassava and maize each merely share under 6% of total production value, while fruits (of which bananas contribute more than half) contributed 14%. Sugar, tobacco, and coffee are the other key crops, all together amounting to almost 10% of agricultural output value. Food crops are grown primarily for home consumption.

Increased investments in irrigation have supported extensive diversification to other crops. In 2019, around 51% of the country's harvested area was devoted to rice production, down from 72% in 1998 (Figure 2.8). Large investments in irrigation systems over the last 2 decades expanded the cropped area to 1,613,935 ha in 2019, but only 28% of this area is irrigated (Table 2.4). Irrigation development focused mainly in the central region which has the largest share of irrigated crop area (37%) in the country. The provinces with the largest irrigated areas are Savannakhet (82,000 ha), Vientiane Province (60,000 ha), Attapu (38,000 ha), and Vientiane Capital (37,000 ha).

Figure 2.7: Lao PDR Gross Agricultural Production Value, 2019

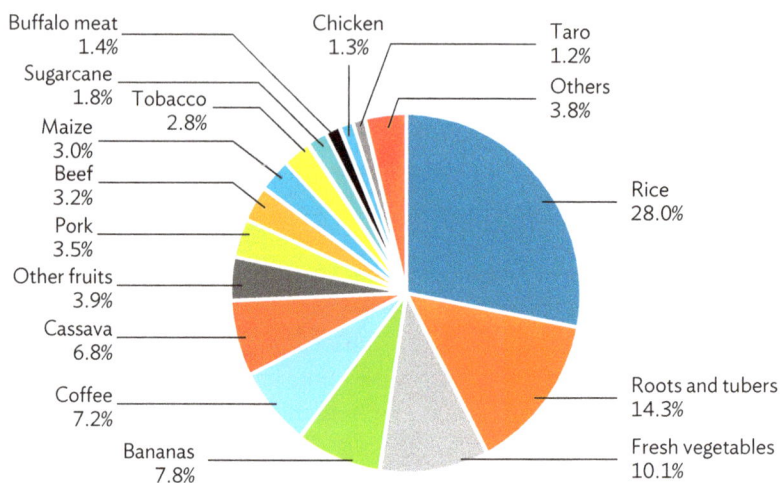

Buffalo meat 1.4%
Sugarcane 1.8%
Maize 3.0%
Beef 3.2%
Pork 3.5%
Other fruits 3.9%
Cassava 6.8%
Coffee 7.2%
Bananas 7.8%
Tobacco 2.8%
Chicken 1.3%
Taro 1.2%
Others 3.8%
Rice 28.0%
Roots and tubers 14.3%
Fresh vegetables 10.1%

Lao PDR = Lao People's Democratic Republic.
Source: Food and Agriculture Organization of the United Nations. FAOSTAT. http://www.fao.org/faostat/en/#data (accessed 11 January 2021).

Figure 2.8: Share of Crops to Total Area Harvested, 1998–2019
(%)

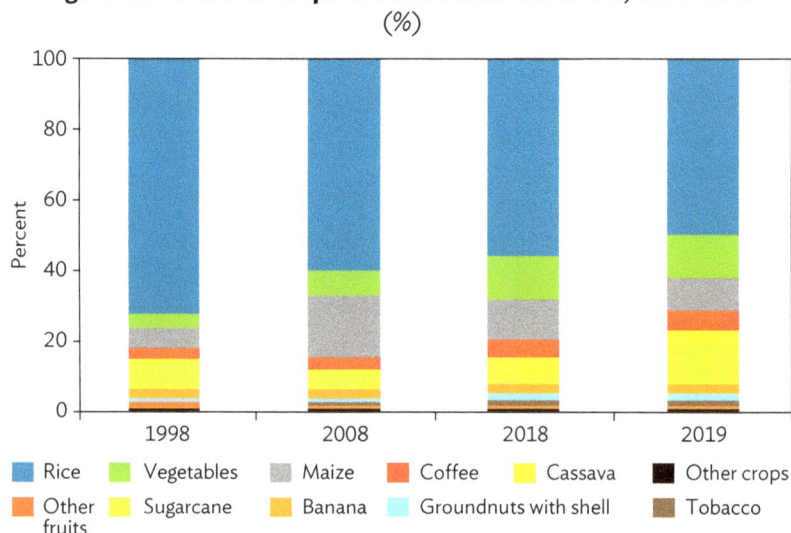

Legend:
- Rice
- Vegetables
- Maize
- Coffee
- Cassava
- Other crops
- Other fruits
- Sugarcane
- Banana
- Groundnuts with shell
- Tobacco

Notes: Other fruits include fresh fruit, watermelons, oranges, tangerines, mandarins, clementines, satsuma, pineapples, papayas, stone fruit, grapefruit including pomelos, other melons including cantaloupe, lemons and limes, mangoes, mangosteens, and guavas.
Source of data: Food and Agriculture Organization of the United Nations (2020); FAOSTAT. http://www.fao.org/faostat/en/#data. (accessed January 2021).

Table 2.4: Total Irrigated Area by Region and Cropping Season, 2019

Region	Total Cropped Area (ha)	Total Irrigated Area (ha)	Wet Season Irrigated Area (ha)	Dry Season Irrigated Area (ha)	Total Share of Irrigated Crop Area (%)
Northern region	528,109	100,465	77,600	22,865	19.0
Central region	665,560	243,825	148,249	95,576	36.6
Southern region	420,296	99,596	53,951	45,645	23.7
Total	**1,613,935**	**443,886**	**279,800**	**164,086**	**27.5**

ha = hectare.
Note: Total share of irrigated crop area was calculated based on total irrigated area over total cropped area then multiplied by 100.
Source: Ministry of Agriculture and Forestry (2020).

Although land devoted to paddy production has remained the largest, more land areas have been converted to producing other crops such as vegetables, maize, coffee, cassava, sugarcane, and bananas in line with the commercialization policy promoted by the government's Agricultural Development Strategy to the year 2025 and Vision to the year 2030. The strategy's emphasis on crop diversification has led to development of agricultural focal areas specializing in plantation crops and high-value crops such as vegetables and fruits. The government's large investment in irrigation facilities, introduction of modern production technologies, development of infrastructure and distribution systems from farm to market have contributed to higher agricultural productivity and have enhanced the country's food security.

The production of non-rice crops such as maize, starchy roots, and coffee has increased over time in several provinces. Maize is the second most important crop in the Lao PDR in terms of area planted. From 2018 to 2019, around 66% (513,578 tons) of the country's total maize production was concentrated in the northern region, particularly in the provinces of Oudomxai (18.3%) and Xaignabouli (16.6%), while the central and southern regions contributed 25.4% and 8.8%, respectively. Maize is grown mainly for human consumption in the central and southern regions and primarily for export and animal feed in the northern region. Starchy roots (e.g., cassava) are another important crop, with harvested areas expanding in all regions—the southern region, for example, increased its production of starchy crops by 18.3 times between 2009 and 2019 (Figure 2.9).

Figure 2.9: Lao PDR Crop Production by Region, 1998–2019

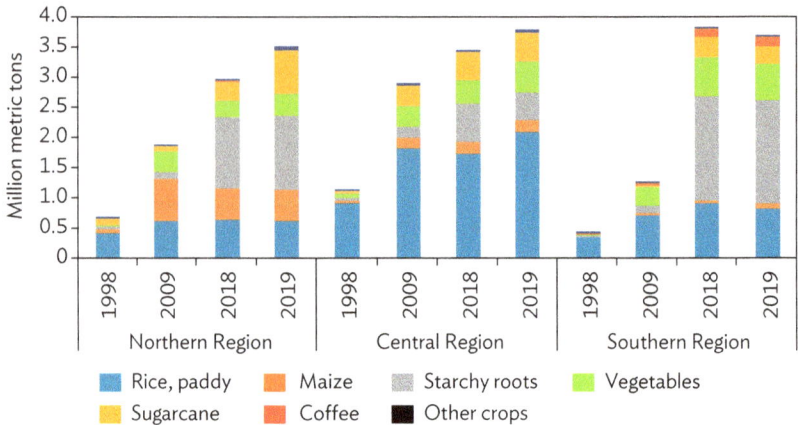

Lao PDR = Lao People's Democratic Republic.
Sources of data: Lao Statistical Information Service. Lao Statistics Bureau. https://laosis.lsb.gov.la/tblInfo/TblInfoList.do (accessed January 2021); National Statistics Centre, Committee for Planning and Investment (2005); and Ministry of Agriculture and Forestry (2020).

In the past years, the coffee sector has drawn more domestic and international investments for its development as a result of the competitiveness it has established in the global market. In 2019, total coffee production in the Lao PDR reached 165,888 tons and provided around $95.5 million to the sector's agricultural gross value output.[10] About 96% of this output comes from the southern region particularly from the provinces of Champasak, Sekong, and Salavan. The Bolaven Plateau is where much of this coffee is grown—which was planted in about 78,875 ha in 2018. In recent years, some major trends have progressively modified the coffee sector such as (i) renewal of plantations and replacement of the robusta variety with arabica in smallholder plantations; (ii) increase in large-scale industrial plantations; and (iii) expansion of coffee areas in the north, particularly in Louangphabang.

Rice production has improved substantially in the last 2 decades; however, various production and operational inefficiencies among its value-chain players have restrained the sector, which needs more public support. Rice production is largely concentrated in the central region which contributed 59% of the country's total rice production in 2019. The central and southern regions produce most of the paddy rice since both regions have predominantly plain lands, in contrast to the challenging topography of the northern region. Savannakhet province is the largest producer of paddy rice (Figure 2.10).

---

[10]   FAO. FAOSTAT. http://www.fao.org/faostat/en/#data (accessed 11 January 2021).

Figure 2.10: Paddy Rice Production by Province, 2005–2019

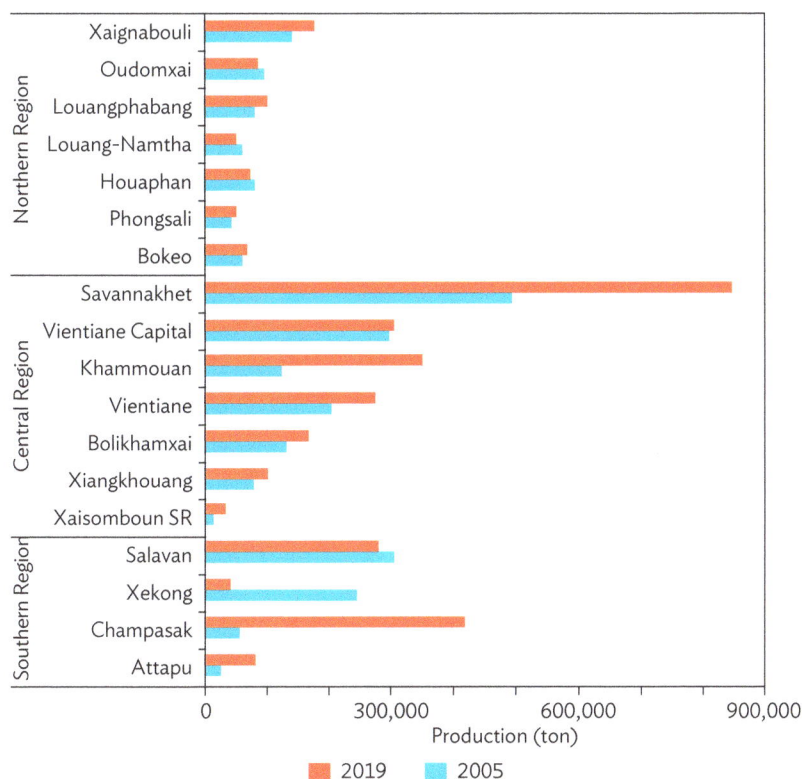

Sources of data: Lao Statistical Information Service. Lao Statistics Bureau. https://laosis.lsb.gov.la/tblInfo/ TblInfoList.do (accessed January 2021; National Statistics Centre, Committee for Planning and Investment (2005); and Ministry of Agriculture and Forestry (2014).

According to a World Bank study (2018a), Lao rice farmers receive a relatively high farm-gate price of paddy, but high production costs usually erode potential profits. Furthermore, the ratio of farm-gate prices to wholesale or retail rice prices in the Lao PDR is the lowest among its peers, which dampens farm supply responses.

Several issues restrain the rice sector in the Lao PDR: (i) low productivity and quality management at the farm and immediate post-farm levels; (ii) a fragmented milling sector dominated by small operators using old technology; (iii) a market system that fails to provide incentives for product quality; and (iv) lack of a significant consumer class with high purchasing power that could foster consolidation of wholesale and retail sectors and reduce costs.

The high cost of paddy production and operational inefficiencies among multiple players in the value chain are responsible for high consumer prices of rice. Many of these constraints are structural and may require some public support to eradicate. It is essential that the government (i) facilitate value-chain linkages between farmers and millers; (ii) enhance access of farmers and millers to finance; and (iii) improve quantity and quality of public services delivery, particularly in areas needing support to acquire new production technologies (for seed, applied research, mechanization, cooperatives/farm clusters, and good agricultural practices, for example) that can reduce production costs and improve product quality for the purpose of commercializing the agriculture sector.

While regulatory or administrative barriers are found to have a minor role in directly inflating the cost structure of the rice value chain, cumbersome regulations that limit entry, affect market structure, and reduce competition should be discouraged. The Lao PDR authorities have recently made efforts to encourage private sector investment in value chains, support the promotion of contract farming, and constrain the use of distortive trade instruments (such as export or cross-provincial bans and/or roadblocks for movement of rice). Lowering regulatory costs for businesses, strengthening enforcement of contracts and product labeling, and removing price regulations for paddy rice have increased private sector investment, fostered competition, created incentives for efficiency improvements, and further contributed to the reduction of costs along the agricultural value chain (see Box 2.2).

Meanwhile, vegetable production has also increased in all regions. It increased steadily from 2005, peaking in 2015–2016 with total production reaching 1.6 million tons. In 2016, the southern region produced more than 50% (856,000 tons) of the vegetables in the Lao PDR. However, in 2017 and 2018, vegetable production declined by about 30% compared with the 2016 production, but later started to increase again in 2019 (Figure 2.11). According to FAO (2020), the area dedicated to vegetable production reached more than 160,000 ha in 2019 due to an increase in contract farming by foreign companies that support farmers with seeds, fertilizers, plastic sheeting, and drip irrigation. Despite the progressive use of new technologies, many vegetable farmers had only an average of 2 *rai*[11] on which to plant vegetables, too small to reap economies of scale. Many farmers still lacked adequate skills for good crop management, particularly in dealing with pest and disease problems, and they have limited access to quality seed varieties. Much of the vegetable value chain production

---

[11]   A *rai* is a unit of area equal to 1,600 square meters (0.16 hectares) and is used in measuring land area for a cadastre or cadastral map.

Box 2.2: The Typical Rice Value Chain in the Lao PDR

The typical segments of the rice value chain in the Lao People's Democratic Republic (Lao PDR) comprise (i) supply inputs, (ii) farm production, (iii) assembly of farm products, (iv) agricultural processing, and (v) marketing through wholesale or retail (Figure B2.2.1). Various private and public input suppliers or agricultural stations, such as seed centers, supply inputs (such as seeds, fertilizers, etc.) and many small and medium-sized farm households carry out production. Increasingly, many small farmers have partnered with local rice mills, which also provide fertilizer on credit and seeds sourced from seed production groups. Inputs are repaid "in kind" during the harvesting season. Paddy assembly is carried out by local collectors or middleman traders, who buy from farmers and deliver to rice mills. In the case of contract farming, many of the millers' collectors are hired on a flat-rate commission basis. However, some farmers who have close connections to the rice mill can directly deliver their harvested rice to the mill. Then the mill processes the rice and distributes the final product to wholesalers and retailers, but not exclusively. Some of the rice mills also directly sell rice at the rice-mill-gate price, while others also facilitate wholesaling of rice directly to big urban markets.

Figure B2.2.1: Segments of the Lao PDR Rice Value Chain

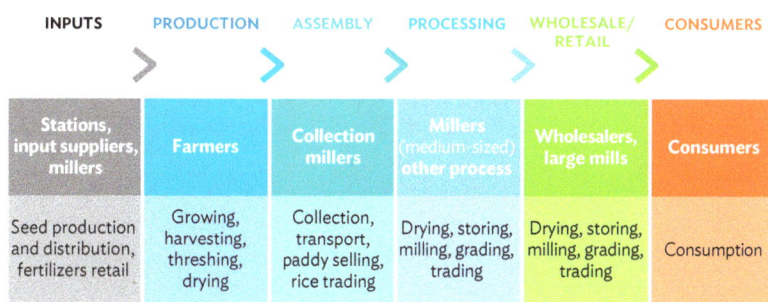

INPUTS	PRODUCTION	ASSEMBLY	PROCESSING	WHOLESALE/ RETAIL	CONSUMERS
Stations, input suppliers, millers	Farmers	Collection millers	Millers (medium-sized) other process	Wholesalers, large mills	Consumers
Seed production and distribution, fertilizers retail	Growing, harvesting, threshing, drying	Collection, transport, paddy selling, rice trading	Drying, storing, milling, grading, trading	Drying, storing, milling, grading, trading	Consumption

Source: Hoppe et al. (2018).

in the Lao PDR still uses customary farming and marketing methods (see Box 2.3). These are some of the factors that contribute to the decline in vegetable quality and productivity in the country (World Bank 2018a).

Organic farming is an emerging niche in Lao PDR agriculture, and the country has a large comparative advantage in the global market. However, production-to-market value chains and quality standards of these products remain underdeveloped. Vegetable farming is a potential growth source for organic

Figure 2.11: Vegetable Production in the Lao PDR by Region, 2005–2019

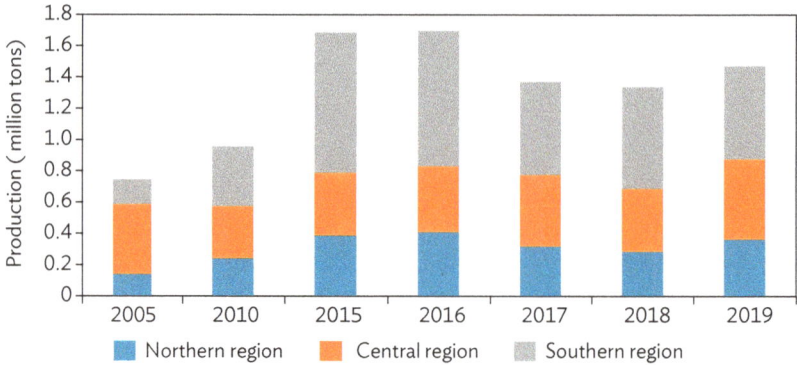

Source: Lao Statistical Information Service. Lao Statistics Bureau. https://laosis.lsb.gov.la/tblInfo/TblInfoList.do (accessed 11 January 2021).

Box 2.3: The Lao PDR Vegetable Value Chain

According to Hoppe et al. (2018), much of the vegetable value chain production in the Lao People's Democratic Republic (Lao PDR) is still very traditional, using customary farming and marketing methods. Farm households often venture into production even with no formal arrangements with traders, and many farmers have inadequate knowledge and understanding of existing government regulations, particularly in the area of food safety.

Vegetable trading involves collectors, wholesalers, and retailers. But vegetables are sold mostly by small retailers in traditional wet markets, with the bulk of the trading done by small-scale and one-person traders, some of whom are the farmers themselves. Collectors assemble the crop in their small trucks and transport it to wholesale markets. The business transaction is generally conducted face-to-face or one-on-one, and payment is made in cash. Wholesalers purchase vegetables from the collectors. Many retailers operate on a small scale and usually sell different types of vegetables in fresh markets around Vientiane Capital. Market offerings are highly dependent on production seasonality, causing vegetable prices to fluctuate sharply throughout the year. Prices peak usually during the early weeks before the harvesting season when overall supply is still low, and drop at harvest time. Imports of vegetables from Thailand are regulated only to fill seasonal gaps when local supplies are insufficient to meet demand.

Source: Hoppe (2018).

produce to supply the emerging local demand and increasing international tourist arrivals. A movement to grow organic produce for the local and tourist markets is emerging in the Lao PDR as evidenced by an ADB survey done in 2019 and 2020 (see Chapter 4). According to a value-chain survey conducted by the World Bank (2018a) in Vientiane, consumers with higher incomes and education levels prefer foods that are compliant with sanitary standards and meet their expectations in terms of taste, packaging, and appearance. These customers are growing in number and are willing to pay more for quality food. Moreover, their demand is driving innovation in processing, packaging, and branding in micro, small, and medium-sized processing enterprises. However, the current state of processing of vegetables in the Lao PDR is very limited mainly due to the lack of knowledge on processing techniques and lack of access to finance. Additionally, lack of suitable labor is a common problem among the country's vegetable farmers and traders.

UNCTAD (2012, 2020) reports that organic coffee is an important niche product of the Lao PDR, accounting for about 71.8% of certified organic land, followed by rice (17.2%), and vegetables and fruits (7.2%). Other agricultural products with organic certification are tea, mulberry (for tea and silk), soybeans, sugarcane, honey, jams, and wine.

Much of the coffee in the Lao PDR is produced in the Bolaven Plateau, on which the provinces of Champasak, Salavan, and Xekong are located. The volume of tea production has also increased significantly in the upland areas of Phongsali and in the plateau areas of Xiangkhouang. Meanwhile, high volumes of organic maize are produced in Bokeo, Oudomxai, Xaignabouli, Xiangkhouang, and Houaphan for export to neighboring countries.

The production of livestock, particularly poultry, has increased, while mechanization has replaced the buffalo as a farm animal. For smallholder households in the rural areas, raising livestock is perceived to be a valuable means of accumulating household savings and storing wealth. They regard livestock as a safety net they can liquidate when they need cash. Livestock plays a valuable role in Lao traditions, particularly for various ethnic groups.

Figure 2.12 shows the increase in livestock production in 1998–2019. The total number of cattle has grown by 87% from 1998 to 2019, especially in the central region, but growth of buffaloes was only 11% from 1998 to 2019. This is due to increased mechanization in agricultural production, replacing the buffalo as a draft animal. The possibility of using buffalo to develop a dairy industry is being explored but as yet is in its infancy.[12] Poultry production increased in all three regions, with the largest expansion in the northern and southern regions (Figure 2.12). Accessibility to markets created greater opportunities for farmers in these two regions to invest in commercial production.

Figure 2.12: Lao PDR Livestock Production by Region, 1998–2019

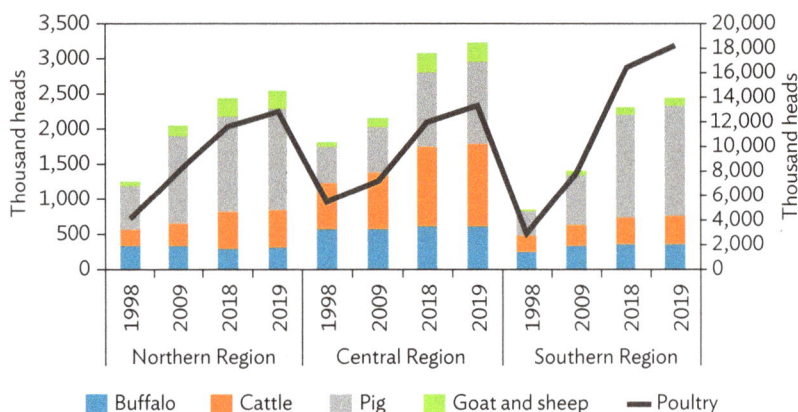

Lao PDR = Lao People's Democratic Republic.
Note: Left-hand side refers to production of buffalo, cattle, pigs, goats, and sheep. Right-hand side refers to chicken production.
Sources of data: Lao Statistical Information Service. Lao Statistics Bureau. https://laosis.lsb.gov.la/tblInfo/TblInfoList.do (accessed January 2021); National Statistics Centre, Committee for Planning and Investment (2005); and Ministry of Agriculture and Forestry (2020).

According to United Nations (UN) COMTRADE data, livestock and dairy products are the fastest growing and largest group of agricultural imports by the Lao PDR. From a low of $6.2 million of net imports in 2005, these products reached a net value of $282 million in 2015, a 45-fold increase in nominal value. Much of the increase can be attributed to imports of live bovine cattle and live swine, which might be associated with the rise in livestock contract farming. Schoenweger et al. (2012) estimated that livestock concessions cover 31,494 hectares, with an average land size of 573 hectares per contract.

The Lao agricultural product and market chains are dominated by isolated farmers and agriculture enterprise operators that are organized in small groups, and often have difficulty in accessing inputs, credit, and technology, which in turn result in lower productivity and income. The lack of functional value chain limits commercialization of agricultural products (Oraboune 2008). Agro-enterprises, farmers, and marketers are unable to effectively link with

---

[12] See, for example, Laos Buffalo Diary. http://www.laosbuffalodiary.com/.

each other, missing opportunities arising from rapidly growing urban, regional, or international markets. The absence of a commercial network makes it more difficult for these agricultural players to gain access to markets and the necessary knowledge to improve quality, add value, and innovate.

Demand for high-value products needs to be created, and necessary incentives to support post-production systems to meet food safety and quality standards need to be in place. Smallholder farmers and agro-enterprises are less able and willing to invest in new technology, infrastructure, production, and processing assets, unless there is demand for high-value quality products. Incentives and support must also be acted upon to develop post-production systems to ensure that Lao products meet the technical, sanitary, and phytosanitary standards necessary to ensure product quality and food safety of agricultural products.

The economy of the Lao PDR has benefited greatly from more than 3 decades of market opening since NEM was introduced in 1986. The value of the country's recorded international trade expanded exponentially in nominal United States (US) dollar terms. Notwithstanding this dramatic achievement, numerous and nontrivial border barriers to international trade are still evident. Table 2.5 reveals that while the Lao PDR's applied import tariffs are about half the rates that were established as the World Trade Organization maximum, they still average 12% for farm products, which is higher than the nonfarm products' average of 7% in 2017.

Certainly, informal or unrecorded trade of some products would effectively lower the extent of protection these tariffs provide to local producers; but other products also face nontariff import restrictions in addition to tariffs. Furthermore, taxes or other restrictions on exports of some farm products lower the average rate of assistance provided to farmers by trade policies. The net effect of these various measures on the Lao PDR has yet to be properly estimated so that a comparison can be made with rates in other Asian countries as reported in, for example, Anderson and Martin (2009).

Early in the reform process, the Lao PDR government was concerned about the country's capacity to maintain food (especially rice) self-sufficiency. Fearing that domestic producers would take up cash crops and livestock farming opportunities rather than produce basic food staples when cheaper rice was flooding in from neighboring countries, the government imposed restrictions to reduce dependence on rice imports. In addition, the government did not allow provinces to ship rice to other provinces until they could produce twice

Table 2.5: Weighted Average MFN Applied Tariff to Agricultural and Nonagricultural Products in the Lao PDR by Key Trading Partner, 2017
(%)

Products	MFN Applied Tariff	Lao PDR Preferential Tariff
Agricultural		
Thailand	46	46
PRC	48	16
European Union	43	43
Viet Nam	16	15
Japan	0.5	0.5
Nonagricultural		
Thailand	0.9	0.9
PRC	3.9	0.8
Viet Nam	1.6	1.5
India	7.8	7.8
European Union	9.9	9.9

Lao PDR = Lao People's Democratic Republic, MFN = most favored nation, PRC = People's Republic of China.
Source: WTO (2019).

as much rice as was consumed there (ADB 2017a). Such price-distorting trade-related policies—whether they help or harm certain groups such as farmers—tend to lower national income and economic growth.

A small amount of rice exports has been recorded since 2014. But rice imports are still relatively small in 2019 (Figure 2.13). The Lao PDR's rice self-sufficiency appears to have been in the 97%–100% range since the 1980s.

Figure 2.13: Lao PDR Rice Import and Export Volumes, 1961–2019

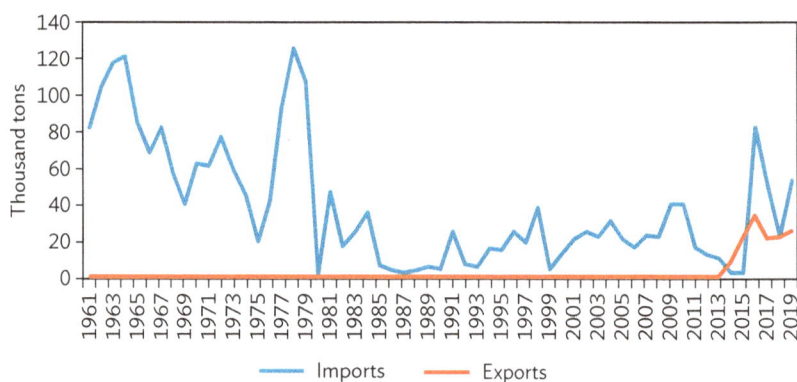

Lao PDR = Lao People's Democratic Republic.
Source of data: Food and Agriculture Organization of the United Nations. FAOSTAT. http://www.fao.org/faostat/en/#data (accessed January 2021).

Linkages between the Agriculture and Tourism Sectors in the Lao PDR

Development of Organic Agricultural Production

Despite having the smallest agricultural area devoted to organic agriculture among other Association of Southeast Asian Nations (ASEAN) member countries, the share of the Lao PDR's certified organic crop area (0.4%) is larger than that of Myanmar and Thailand. The Lao PDR ranked fourth to Viet Nam, the Philippines, and Cambodia in 2018 (Figure 2.14), indicating that organic agriculture has high growth potential. The country's relatively pristine soil, water resources, environment, and low chemical use in farming are natural advantages with regard to organic agriculture.

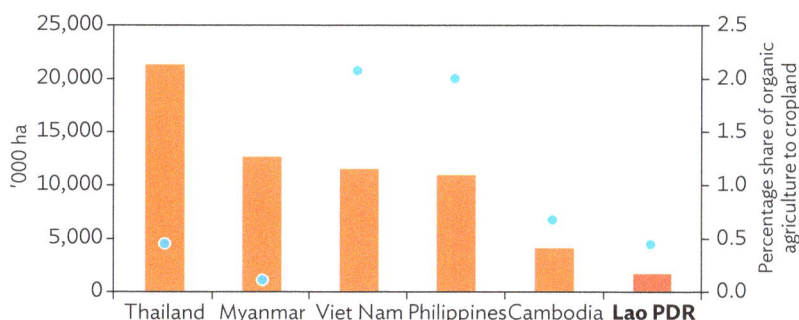

Figure 2.14: ASEAN Cropland and Organic Agriculture, 2018
('000 and %)

ASEAN = Association of Southeast Asian Nations, ha = hectare, Lao PDR = Lao People's Democratic Republic.
Note: Bar graphs refer to crop area in thousand hectares (left axis). Dots refer to percentage share of organic agriculture to cropland (right axis).
Source: Food and Agriculture Organization of the United Nations. FAOSTAT. http://www.fao.org/faostat/en/#data (accessed 11 January 2021).

Promoting organic farming is the government's key strategy to involve rural smallholder producers in market-oriented agriculture. The country's Agriculture Development Strategy to the year 2025 and Vision to the year 2030 encapsulates the goal to develop the organic sector. The plan is to support existing organic markets and establish new ones in Vientiane Capital and the provinces of Savannakhet, Louangphabang, Champasak, Xiangkhouang, Oudomxai, Louang-Namtha, and Vientiane Province by 2020, and in all provinces by 2025. The market share of organic agriculture products is targeted to be 25% of all agricultural produce by 2025. Coffee, rice, and silk are among the organic agricultural crops with export potential. Under the Ministry of Agriculture and Forestry's Development Strategy of the Crop Sector 2025 and Vision 2030 (MAF 2015a), 2% of agricultural land area or about 70,000 farms will be allocated to organic agriculture or certified as organic by 2025.[13]

Agro-Food Processing Industry Development

The food processing sector has remained underdeveloped and dispersed. Households are mostly involved in agro-food processing, which is mainly oriented toward food preservation and small-scale commercialization. With a few exceptions, a large majority of formal processors are very small and highly concentrated. A large number of meat processing companies can be found in Savannakhet and Vientiane provinces and the capital, while most of the vegetable and food preservation processors are gathered in Xaignabouli province. Millers of non-rice or maize grains are generally located in Vientiane, Louangphabang, Champasak, and Oudomxai provinces; noodle production is concentrated in Savannakhet province; and processors of coffee and tea are mostly found in Phongsali, Savannakhet, and Oudomxai (GIZ 2017b). These locally made products or uniquely processed agricultural products serve as an important resource especially for local hotels, shops, and tourism businesses specializing on food tourism.

Ensuring a stable supply of raw materials in the absence of vertical integrators is a challenge, and the presence of intermediaries and consignees in the supply chain raises the cost of obtaining these materials. Also, the domestic market is too small a target for the food processing sector, and processed food imports are deemed cheaper than local products (ERIA 2019). It will be important to selectively identify niche markets particularly those with comparative advantage.

To compete, the agro-processing sector must design policies and implement regulations to ensure compliance with the safety and quality standards required for exports to other countries. The Lao PDR government is already collaborating with different sectors and entrepreneurs to improve the quality of agricultural products for increased export, particularly to the PRC, the country's largest export market. The Lao PDR has successfully met quality standards for crops and related products—such as rice, corn, cassava, bananas, watermelon, and sweet potatoes—exported to the PRC.

---

[13]   Note that the Lao Organic Certification issued by the Lao Certification Body is only used domestically and is not recognized in regional or international markets. Producers who want to export to organic markets abroad need to obtain third-party certification to prove that they meet the organic standards of importing countries.

Emerging Ecotourism Industry[14]

The Lao PDR's tourism industry is growing rapidly. The sector offers enormous opportunities that support inclusive economic growth by stimulating demand and production within, as well as in other sectors. It is an important contributor to job creation, both directly and indirectly through its backward and forward linkages with other economic sectors. Tourism is also perceived as a catalyst in expanding businesses and generating positive impacts such as increased income, output, and employment at local and national levels (Khanal 2011). Some studies say that if linkages between tourism and agriculture are weak, rather than creating synergies, tourism tends to increase reliance in food imports, undermining both local agriculture and foreign exchange earnings. While tourism may increase the cost of production, laborers and landowners tend to benefit from increased wages, higher resource values, and infrastructure improvements. The sourcing of goods locally from the agriculture sector is seen as a positive and beneficial impact of tourism in developing countries such as the Lao PDR. Most national development plans are designed such that tourism will stimulate economic benefits for other sectors, particularly the agriculture sector (Slocum and Curtis 2018).

The country's rich natural resources and cultural heritage can be stimuli for tourism growth. According to the 2017 Assessment, Strategy, and Road Map for Tourism (ADB 2018), the sector has a high potential to drive the country's development of agriculture, natural resources, and rural areas by creating a demand for agricultural products and providing opportunities to develop short-distance value-addition chains for local produce to be marketed and supplied to tourist destinations. Tourism provides business opportunities and creates jobs, especially to the poor and less-skilled in the rural areas. While tourism jobs may not be as regular because of their seasonality, these can provide farm workers extra income between cropping seasons.

Ecotourism in the Lao PDR is also growing, and the government has established broad guidelines for its development. These guidelines emphasize careful capacity management, sustainable use of resources, respect for cultural and natural diversity, and involvement of local communities in the decision-making process. Among others, the Lao PDR has established successful ecotourism initiatives in Louang-Namtha's Nam Ha national protected area (NPA) and Bokeo's Nam Kan NPA (Box 2.4).

---

[14] According to the International Ecotourism Society (https://ecotourism.org/what-is-ecotourism/), ecotourism is defined as responsible travel to natural areas that conserves the environment, sustains the well-being of local people, and involves interpretation and education.

Box 2.4: Economic Impact of the Nam Ha Ecotourism Project on Natural Resource Protection and Rural Development

The Nam Ha Ecotourism Project started in October 1999, with the objective of promoting a community-based ecotourism model to help relieve pressure on the Nam Ha national protected area (NPA), particularly its forest ecosystem. The program helps local communities generate income and employment opportunities. The model is based on a threat assessment methodology in which the NPA management unit identifies and ranks a number of activities that pose direct threats to the ecological integrity of the protected area. It turns out that residents of the NPA themselves have committed some of the identified threats, such as slash-and-burn agriculture, unsustainable harvesting of non-timber forest products for sale and consumption, and illegal wildlife hunting. Outsiders were also found to engage in harmful activities, such as hunting and trade of wildlife. In addition, an increase in the number of free-ranging domestic animals are disturbing wildlife populations by competing for habitat and spreading diseases. Timber harvesting has been rampant. Road construction has also reduced habitats and gave outsiders easy access to illegal hunting and harvesting.

Ecotourism through this program has proved helpful in generating significant revenue for the local communities. Since 1999, community eco-guides and associated service providers have received over $600,000 from the Eco-Guide Service Unit treks alone. This represents significant additional income for a province whose GDP per capita was $389. Tourism has supplemented traditional village livelihoods, allowing community members to diversify their occupations, save money, purchase household items, and pay for school fees. Women who used to spend almost 2 days collecting bamboo or rattan shoots and another day transporting them to market by foot, would earn only about $1–$2 per day. With the program, these women can now spend only 2 to 3 hours to prepare a meal for tourists and earn $3–$6 without having to venture far from the village, thus affording them more time for childcare or other household or economic activities.

In 2006, the Nam Ha Eco-Guide Service Unit sold 359 tours for 1,787 persons, and generated $56,940 in gross revenues for the following:

- Communities and merchants selling food and water on all tours
- Accommodation in villages
- Transportation
- Guide fees
- Handicrafts

Source: UNDP (2012).

Meanwhile, agritourism is another type of program that is expanding. Commonly marketed as "farm-stay" or "community-based tourism," agritourism allows tourists to experience life on a farm. In the Lao PDR, agritourism activities include trekking and farm-stays, and home-stay in the northwest where tourists see the production of mountain rice, livestock, forest foods, and medicinal herbs. In the central region, tourists visit mainly traditional weaving villages with some livestock and rice paddies, while in the southern region, visitors flock to the Bolaven Plateau and large coffee plantations to experience the planting and picking of coffee beans (ASEAN National Tourism Organization 2013). In 2016, the Phutawen Farm (Box 2.5) located in Vientiane Capital began receiving support from international development partners because of its programs to improve farmers' livelihoods (ADB 2018).

Box 2.5: Phutawen Farm – The New Hub of Sustainable Agritourism in the Lao PDR

The Phutawen Farm is located in Ban Hai Village, Pak Ngum District, a 90-minute drive from Vientiane city. It was built to pioneer and promote sustainable food production and serve as an agritourism demonstration model with local community involvement.

More than 2 years was spent on research, preparing a feasibility study, and refining the farm's integrated sustainable agriculture, inclusive business, and tourism concept. In 2016, Phutawen Farm entered into cooperation with the GIZ–ASEAN project on Standards in the Southeast Asian Food Trade to collaborate on the promotion and application of good agricultural practice standards for fruits and vegetables produced in the farm, as well as in the implementation of the Lao organic standard accreditation for their rice and field crops. The farm also serves as a technology and knowledge hub for plant production planning in greenhouses, plant propagation, proper chemical usage, integrated pest management, preharvest and postharvest management, reducing postharvest losses, quality production, and quality management. It also acts as a regional market link between farmers and consumers, while increasing awareness on food safety and quality agricultural products.

Phutawen Farm is open to the public on weekends. Activities include farm tours, cycling, and camping. Visitors can enjoy a combination of agriculture and nature activities such as watching the sunflower and cosmos fields bloom, as well as picking and buying fresh vegetables (ASEAN National Tourism Organization 2013).

Source: GIZ (2017a).

Food has become central to the tourism experience, sparking an interest in promoting it to enhance a particular destination or as a main attraction in a region. From an economic standpoint, food tourism is an opportunity to generate income as tourists tend to be less sensitive to the price of food which makes up one-third of tourism expenditures (Hall et al. 2003).

Conclusion

The economy of the Lao PDR has benefited greatly from more than 3 decades of market opening since NEM was introduced in 1986. Like other countries in Southeast Asia, it has undergone structural transformation from a primarily agrarian economy to a more diversified and market-oriented one. Nevertheless, agriculture remains crucial in fostering inclusive growth in the country, since the sector has the largest employment share in the country (around 70%) and provides income to a large rural population (around 60% of household income is from the sector).

Agriculture and forestry-based production have played a key role in the subsistence and survival of many rural families, providing about 66% of the total rural household income. Food accounts for about 60% of the low-income population's total household expenditure, causing many to be highly vulnerable to food price shocks. Successive national socioeconomic development plans since 1991 have all emphasized the need to focus on developing the agriculture sector, including supporting shifts to nonfood (e.g., livestock) and commercial crop (e.g., maize, sugar, coffee) production while maintaining food sufficiency for the general population. Investments have been made in irrigation to expand cultivated areas, in transport infrastructure to move goods and people more efficiently, and in reforms to the landholding system to improve farm productivity. Security in property rights improve farmers' access to affordable credit, and provides an incentive for them to improve land quality and maximize land productivity.

Overall, the country has comprehensive agricultural policies and robust strategies to develop its agriculture sector; however, a more conscientiously aimed effort and stronger institutional coordination among the various agricultural agencies are needed to turn these policies and strategies into action and bring them to fruition. While there have been significant achievements within the sector, still more work is needed.

Product market chains continue to be dominated by small operators seeking to connect with domestic and neighboring markets. There are still very few large agribusinesses in the Lao PDR. Value additions to the existing agricultural products that farmers produce can directly increase their income and contribute to the economic development of the sector. A functional value chain is important to link farmers with other agri-enterprise players, to gain better access to regional markets and innovations that can help improve the quality and value of various local agricultural products. To improve agricultural value chains, the government needs to focus on some of the following key policy areas.

Enhance efficiency in agricultural production and strengthen linkages among key players of the value chain. The government can act as a facilitator between agricultural producers, consolidators, processors, service providers, and traders. In the organic vegetable value chain, for example, organized smallholder organic producers can be linked to the bigger agro-processing companies in exporting processed organic agricultural products. Clustering of the various value-chain players, especially the farmers, processors, and traders can enhance delivery of research and extension services and simplify business activities and provision of credit. In the rice value chain, expediting contacts between farmer producers and rice millers via public–private partnerships can increase and streamline linkage activities.

Develop an enabling and supportive business-friendly regulatory environment. Agricultural value chains can also benefit from a more supportive business and regulatory framework. Given the Lao PDR's comparative advantage in organic farming, developing organic agricultural certification, inspection, and food safety standards that are acceptable to international markets can broaden markets for the organic agricultural products of the country. Strengthening product labeling regulations can also improve transparency in retail markets, especially in organic product certification.

Increase support toward production-enhancing investments such as mechanization, storage and postharvest facilities, farm-to-market connectivity, and modernization of information, communication, and technology across the agriculture value chain. Provision of production-enhancing investments in agriculture can improve the quality of produce and the capacity of farming activities. In the rice value chain, for instance, investments in agricultural mechanization and modern milling and storage facilities can improve the quality of milled rice and reduce losses. Investments in rural road connectivity is also a production-enhancing investment in agricultural value chains. It lowers the trade costs of getting farm produce to markets, thus raising the farm-gate price—and at the same time potentially lowering the urban consumers' retail price. Although the irrigated area has expanded in the past decades, further investments in irrigation are needed, given that large areas with significant potential for productive cultivation are not yet irrigated. Public and private resources have to be channeled to bring modern technology to the rural areas to spur innovation in agricultural production and processing, harness digital technology to enhance value chains, and expand market access, thus increasing farm productivity and raising rural incomes.

Increase investment in agricultural research development and extension. Public investments in agricultural research development and extension—especially in crop variety improvement—and development of the nutritional content of food staples, would boost the income and nutritional health of both farm and nonfarm households, in turn increasing food self-sufficiency and making food more affordable in local markets. Improved research development and extension on cash crops like coffee can have a high payoff since the country already has established markets abroad.

The Lao PDR's intersectoral linkages remain weak, limiting the growth that can result from the positive synergies these sectors can generate. Tourism and agriculture can stimulate and benefit from each other's progress. While organic food production, agro-food tourism industries, handicrafts, and agro-processing of local food products have emerged as employment and income sources, these will need support to bring better opportunities for local producers and farmers and to achieve more inclusive growth. To strengthen the link between these two sectors, the government can build partnership and community by developing a platform that provides incentives and creates a string of networks connecting various agricultural growers, suppliers, and tourism service providers.

CHAPTER 3

Navigating Growth in Lao PDR Tourism

Steven Schipani, Takashi Yamano, and Manisha Pradhananga

People's innate affinity for novel experiences, rising personal incomes, easy access to travel information, and rapidly improving connectivity all drive global tourism growth. With its outstanding tourism resources and strategic location in the world's most populous region, the Lao People's Democratic Republic (Lao PDR) is well-positioned to benefit more from its growing tourism industry. International tourist arrivals rose from 2.5 million in 2010 to 4.8 million in 2019 and corresponding international tourism receipts increased from $381.7 million to $934.7 million over the same period. Tourism's direct contribution to gross domestic product (GDP) was 5.1% and total contribution about 10% in 2019. It is estimated that tourism in the Lao PDR sustains 348,700 (10.2 % of total employment) jobs in a range of service and productive enterprises (WTTC 2021).

Well-managed tourism creates good jobs and economic opportunities for women, youth, and other vulnerable groups. In 2019, tourism sustained up to 334 million jobs worldwide (10% of global employment), mainly in small and medium-sized enterprises (WTTC 2021). Women comprise 60%–70% of accommodation workers but are underrepresented in higher-paying management roles. Southeast Asian countries employ some of the highest percentages of women and people from vulnerable groups. For example, women make up about 70% of Viet Nam's tourism workforce, followed by the Lao PDR (63%) and the Philippines (58%).

The government, the private sector, and civil society increasingly recognize that well-managed tourism uses natural resources sustainably and can contribute substantially to socioeconomic progress. Sustainable Development Goals (SDG) 8, 12, and 14 explicitly uphold global commitments to foster sustainable tourism that creates jobs and promotes local culture and products, sustainably uses marine resources to increase tourism's economic benefits for small island developing states and least developed countries, and monitor tourism's development impacts. Intelligently managed tourism has an important role in attaining most SDGs, particularly those that aim to end poverty and inequality, achieve gender equality, build resilient infrastructure, make cities more inclusive, protect biodiversity, and promote peace (see Box 3.1). This section provides data and discussions that may be useful for the Lao PDR government to develop practical and effective policy actions toward achieving these goals.

Box 3.1: The Contribution of Well-Managed Tourism to Select Sustainable Development Goals

1 NO POVERTY

Tourism fosters inclusive economic growth, generating jobs and income. Tourism development can be linked with national poverty reduction goals, promote entrepreneurship and small businesses, and empower disadvantaged groups, particularly youth and women.

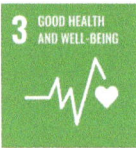

3 GOOD HEALTH AND WELL-BEING

Taxes and other public income generated by tourism can be reinvested in health-care services and other public goods to improve residents' well-being and improve visitor experiences.

5 GENDER EQUALITY

Tourism offers women opportunities to unlock their potential as entrepreneurs, managers, and leaders. It empowers women by providing jobs, income-generating opportunities, and a stronger voice in community decision-making.

8 DECENT WORK AND ECONOMIC GROWTH

Tourism drives economic growth and prosperity, employing about 10% of the global workforce. It creates decent work opportunities, particularly for youth and women, and a pathway for lifelong skills and professional development.

9 INDUSTRY, INNOVATION AND INFRASTRUCTURE

Tourism relies on good public and private infrastructure and innovation, which benefits residents and visitors. It can also incentivize destinations to adopt resource-efficient and clean industrial policies as a means to attract tourists and investment.

Continued next page

Box 3.1 continued

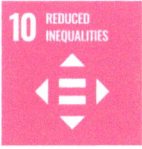

10 REDUCED INEQUALITIES — Tourism reduces regional inequality by providing a means for people to prosper in their place of origin. Tourism can contribute to economic growth in lagging areas and narrow the urban–rural development gap.

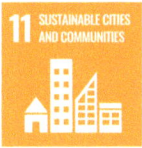

11 SUSTAINABLE CITIES AND COMMUNITIES — Tourism catalyzes urban infrastructure improvements, greenspace development, universal accessibility, urban renewal, and cultural and natural heritage preservation. Tourism can encourage host communities and visitors to reduce the use of plastic, improve solid waste management, and protect the environment.

14 LIFE BELOW WATER — Tourism can raise funds and awareness to protect marine and freshwater ecosystems and biodiversity.

15 LIFE ON LAND — Tourism can raise funds and awareness to protect terrestrial ecosystems, landscapes, and biodiversity.

16 PEACE, JUSTICE AND STRONG INSTITUTIONS — Tourism fosters multicultural and interfaith tolerance and understanding, laying the foundation for more peaceful societies. Tourism can also provide community livelihoods and strengthen cultural identities, helping to prevent violence and conflict.

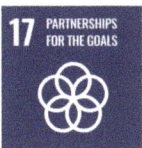

17 PARTNERSHIPS FOR THE GOALS — Tourism is a multisector economic activity that can strengthen international, national, and local stakeholder engagement and cooperation to achieve the SDGs and other common goals.

Source: Adapted by the authors from UNWTO (2019).

Global Tourism Context

In 2018, international tourist arrivals worldwide reached 1.4 billion, 5.6% more than in 2017. International arrivals increased further to 1.5 billion in 2019 before this upward trend was interrupted by the coronavirus disease (COVID-19) pandemic beginning in the first half of 2020 (UNWTO 2020).

Remarkably, about 80% of international travel is intraregional and 78% is for leisure. Before the onset of COVID-19, Europe accounted for 50.8% of international arrivals worldwide, followed by Asia and the Pacific (24.4%) and the Americas (15.5%). Asia and the Pacific's 6.1% international arrivals growth in 2018 outperformed growth in Europe (5.7%) and the Americas (2.9%) and is expected to remain above the global average through 2030.

The People's Republic of China (PRC) is the world's top supplier of international tourists. In 2019, 149.7 million outbound Chinese tourists spent $277.3 billion—more than double that of the United States ($126.0 billion), the world's second highest spending outbound source market that year. Worldwide, average spending per international arrival is $1,010, while the average for emerging economies is $790 per arrival (2017). In 2018, total international tourism receipts reached $1.4 trillion.

Despite tourism's downturn in 2020, historic trends suggest that international and domestic tourism will bounce back and continue to foster global prosperity once COVID-19 is controlled. International and domestic tourism directly contributed $2.7 trillion (3.2%) to global GDP in 2018, mainly from economic activity related to accommodations, food and beverages, retail, transport, and recreation services. The total contribution to global GDP is estimated at $8.8 trillion (10.4%) when capital investment, government spending, and supply chain effects are included.

Tourism in Southeast Asia

Tourism is a major contributor to Southeast Asia's rising prosperity and economic integration. International tourist arrivals grew 7.5% in 2018, reaching 135.2 million (9.5% of 1.4 billion arrivals worldwide), 33.3% more than 2014 (Table 3.1). International arrivals increased further to 143.5 million in 2019, before the COVID-19 pandemic stopped most international travel in early 2020. Pre–COVID-19, tourism-related services together with capital investment, government spending, and supply chain effects contributed in total 12.0% to Southeast Asia's combined GDP and sustained 42.6 million jobs (about 13% of total employment). Domestic tourism generated about half of total tourist spending, with more than 800 million trips per year (WTTC 2020).

Table 3.1: Southeast Asia's Tourist Arrivals, GDP Share, and Employment, 2014–2019

Country	International Tourist Arrivals (million)						Share in 2019 (%)	Change 2014 vs 2019 (%)	Domestic Tourists 2018 (million)	GDP Share 2019 (%)	Jobs (Total Employment) 2019 ('000)
	2014	2015	2016	2017	2018	2019					
Brunei Darussalam	0.2	0.2	.2	.3	.3	.3	0.2	66.6	...	5.4	14.3
Cambodia	4.5	4.8	5.0	5.6	6.2	6.6	4.6	46.9	10	25.7	2,295.9
Indonesia	9.4	10.4	11.5	14.0	15.8	16.1	11.2	70.6	264	5.8	13,180.4
Lao PDR	**4.2**	**4.7**	**4.2**	**3.9**	**4.2**	**4.8**	**3.3**	**15.4**	**2.8**	**10.4**	**348.7**
Malaysia	27.4	25.7	26.8	26.0	25.9	26.1	18.2	-4.7	205.4	11.5	2,279.8
Myanmar	3.1	4.7	2.9	3.4	3.6	4.4	3.0	41.7	7.1	6.9	1,414.9
Philippines	4.8	5.4	6.0	6.6	7.1	8.3	5.8	71.0	97	23.9	9,571.3
Singapore	15.1	15.2	16.4	17.4	18.5	19.1	13.3	26.6	...	10.5	538.5
Thailand	24.8	29.9	32.5	35.6	38.2	39.8	27.7	60.5	160	19.6	8,047.2
Viet Nam	7.9	7.9	10.0	12.9	15.5	18.0	12.6	128.8	80	8.9	4,910.8
Total	**101.4**	**108.9**	**115.6**	**125.7**	**135.2**	**143.5**	**100**	**41.5**	**826.3**	**12.0**	**42,601.8**

... = data not available, GDP = gross domestic product, Lao PDR = Lao People's Democratic Republic
Note: GDP share is for total contribution of tourism.
Sources: National tourism organizations; World Travel & Tourism Council travel and tourism economic impact reports.

Tourism in Southeast Asia is strongly influenced by intraregional travel. There were 51.5 million intraregional tourists in 2019 (35.9% of the total). Other major source markets are the PRC, comprising 22.5% of total visitors, the Republic of Korea (7.3%), and Japan (3.9%).

Enabling policies and quality gateway infrastructure make Southeast Asia one of the world's best-connected tourism destinations. For example, progressive implementation of the Association of Southeast Asian Nations (ASEAN) Multilateral Agreement for the Full Liberalization of Passenger Air Services helped to increase scheduled air-seat capacity from 200 million seats in 2008 to nearly 530 million in 2018. The United Nations World Tourism Organization (UNWTO) ranks Southeast Asia most open in terms of tourist visa requirements, with the ASEAN Framework Agreement on Visa Exemption allowing ASEAN nationals visa-free travel to other ASEAN member countries. In 2019, about one-third of the world population could obtain a tourist visa on arrival, and 26% were not required to obtain a visa when traveling for tourism (UNWTO 2014).

The ASEAN Mutual Recognition Agreement on Tourism Professionals eases labor mobility for workers in 32 job types and provides a framework to improve regional service quality. Growing adoption of ASEAN clean city, green hotel, and other common tourism standards demonstrates the region's firm commitment to improve environmental and social sustainability. The ASEAN common tourism standards platform also provides a venue to develop common health and hygiene standards needed to protect public health and rebuild consumer confidence to travel.

While regional cooperation and facilitative policies could quicken Southeast Asia's tourism recovery once COVID-19 is contained and borders reopen, the generally low competitiveness rankings in Table 3.2 show that significant public and private infrastructure, technology, and human development investments are needed to reinvigorate growth and ensure it is managed inclusively and sustainably.

Table 3.2: Southeast Asia's Travel and Tourism Competitiveness Rankings, 2019

Country	Infrastructure			Enabling Conditions			
	Air Transport	Ground and Ports	Tourist Services	ICT Readiness	Environmental Sustainability	Business Environment	Human Resources and Labor Market
Brunei Darussalam	54	51	74	43	96	46	69
Cambodia	91	111	93	101	139	122	95
Indonesia	38	66	98	67	135	50	44
Lao PDR	**90**	**110**	**89**	**112**	**122**	**75**	**67**
Malaysia	25	27	57	44	105	11	15
Myanmar	...	...	...	...	...	...	...
Philippines	59	93	85	82	103	80	37
Singapore	7	2	36	15	61	2	5
Thailand	22	72	14	49	130	37	27
Viet Nam	50	84	106	83	121	67	47

... = data not available, ICT = information and communication technology, Lao PDR = Lao People's Democratic Republic.
Notes: Rank = 1–140. Lower number indicates better performance.
Source: World Economic Forum (2019).

The ASEAN Tourism Strategic Plan 2016–2025, endorsed by the Lao PDR, guides regional tourism cooperation in Southeast Asia. It sets out an ambitious vision for sustainable and inclusive tourism that contributes significantly to socioeconomic well-being. Strategic directions focus on enhancing tourism competitiveness, promoting the region as a single destination, and ensuring tourism is sustainable and inclusive. There are strategic programs to improve (i) marketing; (ii) product diversification; (iii) investment promotion; (iv) human development; (v) ASEAN tourism standards implementation; (vi) infrastructure; (vii) travel facilitation; (viii) tourism value chain participation; (ix) safety, security, and heritage protection; and (x) environmental protection and climate change responsiveness. The ambitious plan anticipates that by 2025 tourism could contribute 15% to Southeast Asia's combined GDP and support 7% of the region's jobs (ASEAN 2015).

Centrally located in the six-country Greater Mekong Subregion (GMS), the Lao PDR cooperates closely with its neighbors to jointly promote intraregional tourism. The GMS Tourism Sector Strategy 2016–2025 steers these efforts in alignment with ASEAN's vision for more sustainable and inclusive tourism (Mekong Tourism Coordinating Office 2016).[15] Particularly relevant in a post COVID-19 world, GMS tourism cooperation emphasizes the need to build resilience and partnerships to achieve competitive, balanced, and sustainable tourism destination development. Strategic programs to strengthen human resources, improve public infrastructure for tourism, enhance visitor experience and services, support creative marketing and promotion, and facilitate regional travel are estimated to cost $58.7 billion. Crosscutting themes include gender equality, private sector development, environmental sustainability, universal access, and integrated destination management. The GMS Tourism Sector Strategy targets 95 million international visitors, $130 billion annual international visitor expenditure, and 15 million tourism workers (50% women) by 2025. The Lao PDR's recently formulated National Tourism Development Plan 2021–2025 aligns with regional objectives to promote green and sustainable high-quality nature and culture-based tourism that contributes to poverty reduction and inclusive economic growth.

Tourism in the Lao PDR

The government and the private sector work together to entice more tourists, for instance, by organizing "Visit Laos Year" 2018, which helped increase international arrivals by 8.2% that year. However, the Lao PDR's 2010–2019

---

[15]   The GMS comprises Cambodia, the PRC's Yunnan Province and Guangxi Zhuang Autonomous Region, the Lao PDR, Myanmar, Thailand, and Viet Nam.

cumulative annual growth rate of 6.7% slightly lags behind Southeast Asia's 6.9% annual growth rate during this period. Like other destinations across the world, the Lao PDR also witnessed a significant decline of international tourist arrivals (–81.5%) in 2020 as a result of the COVID-19 pandemic.

The Lao PDR's main source of tourism markets are the Southeast Asian countries, which accounted for 66.8% of international arrivals in 2019. Arrivals from the other Asia and Pacific countries totaled 27.5%, followed by Europe (3.8%) and the Americas (1.7%). Arrivals from Africa and the Middle East comprise less than 1% market share. Thailand is the Lao PDR's top source market with about 2.2 million annual arrivals, but its share has declined from 49.6% of the total in 2015 to 45.1% in 2019. Tourists from Viet Nam comprise 19.3% of total arrivals, the PRC 21.3%, and the Republic of Korea 4.2%. Overall, an astonishing 94.3% of the Lao PDR's international tourist arrivals are intraregional (i.e., from Southeast Asia and the rest of Asia and the Pacific). The fastest growing markets within the region, from a base of at least 25,000 arrivals in 2019 were the PRC (26.9%), the Republic of Korea (16.5%), and Thailand (11.9%). In 2019, arrivals from the United States increased 24.4% to 61,184, the highest among the long-haul North American and European markets. The sizable population of Lao-Americans (246,000) partially explains strong growth from the United States (US Department of Commerce, Bureau of the Census 2013).

Tourist Visa Policy

Open tourist visa policies favor Southeast Asia and some north Asian markets. The Lao PDR is a signatory to the ASEAN Framework Agreement on Visa Exemption, allowing ASEAN nationals holding a passport visa-free entry for 14–30 days. Tourists holding a passport from Japan, Luxembourg, the Republic of Korea, the Russian Federation, and Switzerland may enter without a visa for 15 days. Nationals of more than 180 countries can obtain prearranged 30-day tourist visas or visa on arrival at 22 entry ports, with visa fees ranging from $30 to $42. Visa-on-arrival processing typically takes 15–30 minutes at international airports but may be twice as long at busy land ports during peak arrival times. Introduction of electronic visas in 2019 shortened entry processing times for visitors from 150 countries that are eligible for this type of visa.

To attract higher-spending visitors, the Lao PDR should expand visa exemption policies to countries with high outbound tourism expenditure. The PRC, the source market with the most tourist spending in 2018, could potentially supply more tourists to the Lao PDR if visa fees are waived, in the same way that the Republic of Korea and Japan were encouraged to do so (Table 3.3). According to UNWTO and the World Travel & Tourism Council (WTTC), visa exemptions generate higher arrivals growth compared with electronic visa or visa-on-arrival policies. Case studies comparing visa exemption with other forms of visa facilitation show that arrivals growth is 5.3% higher when visa requirements are eliminated (UNWTO and WTTC 2014).

Table 3.3: Lao PDR's Tourist Visa Requirements for High-Spending Source Markets, 2019

Country	Population (million)	Global Tourism Expenditure ($ billion)	Rank	Tourist Visa Required	Arrivals to the Lao PDR Total	Arrivals to the Lao PDR % total
PRC	1,392.7	277.3	1	Yes	1,022,727	21.3
United States	326.8	126.0	2	Yes	61,184	1.3
Germany	82.9	95.6	3	Yes	25,346	0.5
United Kingdom	66.5	70.9	4	Yes	31,976	0.7
France	67.1	48.9	5	Yes	44,416	0.9
Australia	25.0	37.0	6	Yes	24,750	0.5
Canada	37.1	34.5	8	Yes	12,873	0.3
Russian Federation	144.5	34.3	9	No	12,054	0.3
Republic of Korea	51.6	35.1	7	No	203,191	4.2
Italy	60.4	30.1	10	Yes	7,330	0.2
Singapore	5.6	26.5	11	No	11,730	0.2
India	1,352.6	21.3	14	Yes	8,152	0.2
Japan	126.5	20.2	16	No	41,736	0.9
Philippines	106.7	11.9	28	No	17,187	0.4
Malaysia	31.5	12.1	26	No	28,321	0.6
Thailand	69.4	12.1	27	No	2,160,300	45.1
Indonesia	267.7	10.3	33	No	5,161	0.1
Viet Nam	95.5	6.1	43	No	924,875	19.3

Lao PDR = Lao People's Democratic Republic, PRC = People's Republic of China.
Note: Expenditure data and population data are for 2018.
Sources: UNWTO. Tourism Dashboard. https://www.unwto.org/unwto-tourism-dashboard (accessed 6 July 2021); MICT (2020); and population data from World Bank. World Development Indicators Database. https://databank.worldbank.org (accessed 6 July 2021).

Purpose of Visit and Travel Patterns

The main purpose of visit for all source markets is leisure (81.0%), followed by business (7.4%) and visiting family and friends (3.3%). About 63% of international tourists mention they visit the Lao PDR because of its cultural attractions, 59% seek nature-based experiences, and 44% are interested in historic attractions. Religious pilgrimage is another significant motivation to visit. About 37% of international tourists visit Buddhist temples and other monuments, mostly during the November to April festive season.

International tourists predominantly enter the Lao PDR through one of its 24 international land ports (83.5% in 2019) and the rest enter through airports. Land ports are served by international coach services that connect the Lao PDR with neighboring Cambodia, the PRC, Thailand, and Viet Nam. The Mekong River cruising between Chiang Rai in Thailand and Louangphabang in the Lao PDR is another way through which international tourists enter or leave the country, however the recent completion of an expressway between Vientiane Capital and Vangviang has led to a sharp increase in self-driven tourism. Expansion of this expressway further north to the PRC border, and a planned expressway connecting Vientiane Capital with the Lao PDR's southern provinces, is also expected to boost domestic tourism. Domestic overland travel is mainly by interprovincial bus and hired vehicles. The Lao PDR–PRC railway, currently under construction, will provide another important alternative to enter the country, especially for tourists from the PRC (see Box 3.2) (Keola 2019).

Box 3.2: Lao People's Democratic Republic–PRC Railway

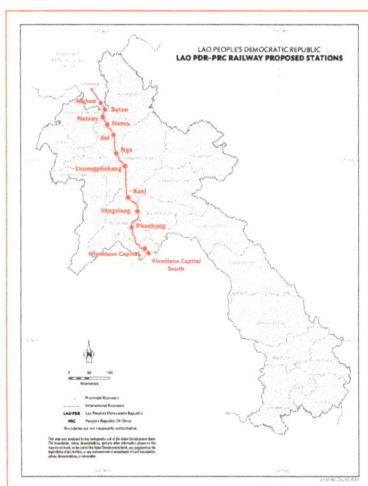

Source: ESCAP and UNCTAD (2019).

The 414-kilometer (km) Lao People's Democratic Republic (Lao PDR)–People's Republic of China (PRC) railway will run from the Lao PDR's Boten border gate in northern Louang-Namtha province to Vientiane Capital, with 10 passenger stations in Louang-Namtha, Oudomxai, Louangphabang, Vientiane Province (including Vangviang district), and Vientiane Capital. Construction started in 2016 and is scheduled for completion by December 2021. The railway is part of the larger Kunming, PRC to Singapore regional rail network and is expected to initially carry about 4 million passengers per year. With an operating speed of 160 km per hour, overland travel time between Vientiane Capital and Louangphabang will be reduced to about 2 hours. Overland travel between the Boten border gate and Louangphabang will also be about 2 hours. The railway is expected to significantly boost Thai and Chinese tourist arrivals, as well as domestic tourism. It will also lower transport

Continued next page

Box 3.2 continued

costs; thus, apart from benefiting the tourism sector, it could make production and export of manufactured goods and agricultural products more competitive.

Destinations served by the railway should proactively prepare for an expected surge in international and domestic tourists. This includes improving local transport infrastructure, environmental services, and tourism destination management capacity. While most Lao tourism businesses have a good understanding of Thai and domestic tourist preferences due to cultural and linguistic similarities, their understanding of the large, diverse, and relatively new Chinese market is low. Lao businesses that want to engage Chinese tourists should become acquainted with the interests and purchasing habits of this potential market segment and target it appropriately. Properly designed Chinese-language digital marketing materials distributed using online resources such as WeChat, Trip.com, and custom-built websites are essential to steer potential customers to local businesses. Other important considerations are to train staff to speak Mandarin, offer Union Pay, Alipay, and WeChat payment options, and ensure free Wi-Fi is available for guests to easily share experiences directly from the destination.

Sources: Authors; and Yap (2017).

Vientiane Capital's Wattay International Airport is capable of handling wide-body jet aircraft and received 574,137 international arrivals or 12.0% of the total in 2019. This is only about 25% of the airport's 2.3 million international passenger handling capacity. In the same year, Louangphabang International Airport, which was recently upgraded to handle larger aircraft, recorded 202,159 arrivals equal to about 4.2% of the country's total.[16] Pakxe and Savannakhet international airports in southern Lao PDR each receive less than 1% of total international arrivals (Figure 3.1). As shown in Table 3.4, both flight frequency and seat capacity increased at a faster pace than the international tourist arrivals during 2017–2019.

The busiest land port of entry is the first Lao–Thai Friendship Bridge near Vientiane Capital, which processed 1.3 million arrivals in 2019 (27.6% of the total). Other main ports of entry are Boten bordering the PRC (536,906 arrivals); Savannakhet's second Lao–Thai Friendship Bridge (405,031 arrivals); Savannakhet's other international land port Dane Savanh bordering Viet Nam (236,403 arrivals); and Champasak's Vang Tao bordering

---

[16] Louangphabang International Airport was upgraded during 2012–2013, enabling it to handle narrow-body jet aircraft.

Table 3.4: Lao PDR Flight Frequency and Seat Capacity, 2017–2019

Origin	2017	2018	2019	% Change 2017–2019
Flight Frequency				
Thailand	4,091	4,515	5,217	27.5
PRC	2,219	2,767	2,422	9.1
Viet Nam	1,613	1,617	1,576	(2.3)
Republic of Korea	1,299	1,773	1,159	(10.8)
Cambodia	984	948	994	1.0
Malaysia	365	259	157	(57.0)
Singapore	197	168	147	(25.4)
Total	**10,768**	**12,047**	**11,672**	**8.4**
Seat Capacity				
Thailand	559,644	616,135	732,445	30.9
PRC	339,130	423,367	440,756	30.0
Republic of Korea	225,429	316,652	187,187	(17.0)
Viet Nam	193,068	219,774	223,191	15.6
Cambodia	122,452	145,968	151,795	24.0
Malaysia	65,700	46,620	28,260	(57.0)
Singapore	28,766	25,224	25,590	(11.0)
Total	**1,534,189**	**1,793,740**	**1,789,224**	**16.6**

( ) = negative, Lao PDR = Lao People's Democratic Republic, PRC = People's Republic of China.
Source: OAG via Pacific Asia Travel Association mPower. https://mpower.pata.org/aviation/flight-frequency (accessed 4 May 2019).

Thailand (206,030 arrivals) (Figure 3.1). The number of Lao outbound travelers that transited land ports reached about 2.7 million in 2019, a 16.1% drop from 2018. Thailand is the most popular destination.

There are distinct central, northern, and southern subnational destination clusters in parts of the country. The central cluster received around 2.2 million international tourists in 2019 understandably because it includes Vientiane Capital and Wattay International Airport. The northern cluster had more than 1.9 million international visitors, with Louangphabang being the main attraction. The southern cluster (Khammouan, Savannakhet, and Champasak provinces) received slightly more than 2.1 million visitors in 2019. During 2014–2019, arrivals increased 108.8% in the northern cluster, 3.0% in the central cluster, and 4.1% in the southern cluster. Arrivals in the southern cluster were 14.1% lower in 2018 compared with 2019 because of fewer Thai tourists and lackluster growth from other source markets.

Figure 3.1: Tourist Arrivals at Port of Entry, 2019
('000 visitors)

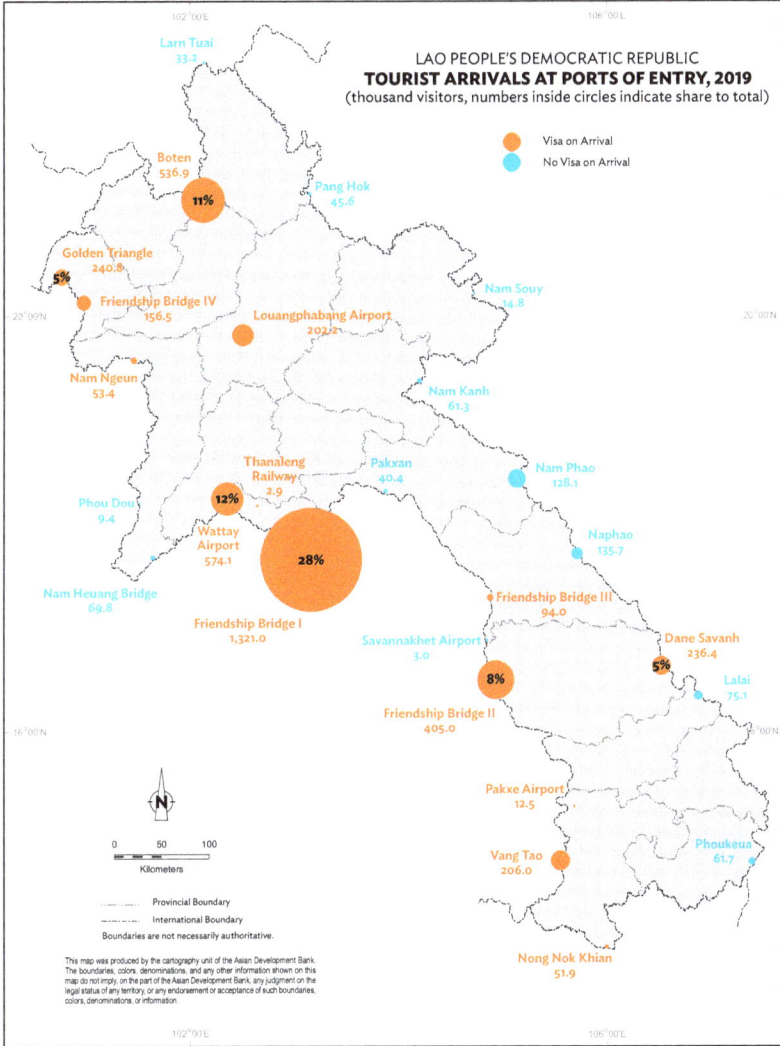

LAO PEOPLE'S DEMOCRATIC REPUBLIC
TOURIST ARRIVALS AT PORTS OF ENTRY, 2019
(thousand visitors, numbers inside circles indicate share to total)

Visa on Arrival
No Visa on Arrival

Larn Tuai 33.1
Boten 536.9 — 11%
Pang Hok 45.6
Golden Triangle 240.8 — 5%
Friendship Bridge IV 156.5
Louangphabang Airport 202.2
Nam Souy 4.8
Nam Ngeun 53.4
Nam Kanh 61.3
Thanaleng Railway 2.9 — 12%
Pakxan 40.4
Nam Phao 128.1
Phou Dou 9.4
Wattay Airport 574.1 — 28%
Naphao 135.7
Nam Heuang Bridge 69.8
Friendship Bridge III 94.0
Friendship Bridge I 1,321.0
Savannakhet Airport 3.0 — 8%
Dane Savanh 236.4 — 5%
Lalai 75.1
Friendship Bridge II 405.0
Pakxe Airport 12.5
Vang Tao 206.0
Phoukeua 61.7
Nong Nok Khian 51.9

Provincial Boundary
International Boundary
Boundaries are not necessarily authoritative.

Source: Authors based on MICT (2020).

The number of domestic tourists increased by 13.1% from about 2.1 million in 2014 to 2.4 million in 2019. Domestic tourists tend to vacation and join festivals in the same subnational destination clusters as international tourists, however, obligations to visit family and friends also strongly motivate domestic travel. In 2019, about 0.5 million domestic tourists visited the central cluster, up to 20.5% from 2014. Domestic tourist arrivals in the northern cluster only slightly increased by 6.0% to 0.31 million in 2019 from 0.30 million in 2014. The southern cluster was the second most popular destination for domestic tourists in 2019 receiving about 0.9 million, a 1.5% increase from 2014.

The Lao PDR's tropical monsoon climate influences tourist arrival patterns. The peak tourism season, when demand for labor and services are highest, occurs during the cool dry period from November through February, with fewer international arrivals in the hot dry months of March and April, and during the rainy season months of May through September. These trends complement the agricultural cycle, as workers can switch to farming activities during the productive rainy season, when there is a decrease in tourism arrivals.

Figure 3.2 shows that in 2019, tourist arrivals averaged 399,255 per month: highest in November (473,648) and lowest in January (331,524). Long-haul international arrivals peaked in June (175,014) and were lowest in April (35,378), a difference of 79.8% between the peak and low seasons. In comparison, intraregional arrivals vary only 51.9% from peak to low season months, ranging from 193,632 in June to 402,665 in November.

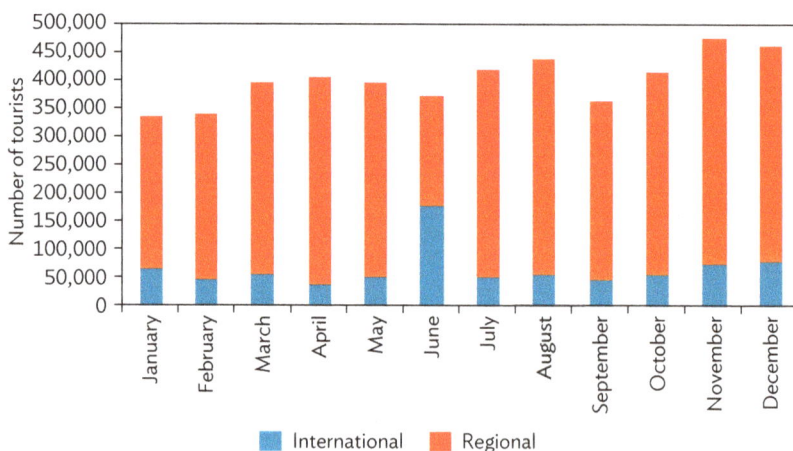

Figure 3.2: Tourist Arrivals by Month and Type of Visitor, 2019

Source: MICT (2019).

Tourism Receipts and Investment

According to the Ministry of Information, Culture and Tourism (MICT), international tourism receipts were $934.7 million in 2019 (Table 3.5). Tourism's direct contribution to GDP was 5.1% and total contribution was about 10% the same year. International tourist spending is among the Lao PDR's main sources of foreign exchange, trailing mineral exports ($1.4 billion), receipts from other industries (nearly $1.3 billion), and electricity exports ($1.3 billion). However, receipts per international tourist average only $195.1, the lowest in Southeast Asia and significantly lower than Asia and the Pacific's $1,220 benchmark. Moreover, substantial amounts of foreign exchange generated by tourism "leak" out of the Lao economy to purchase imported goods and services that are consumed by tourists (ADB 2017b). Accommodation and meals each comprise about 25% of tourist expenditures, followed by shopping (15%) and transport (14%). The remaining 21%, categorized as other expenditures, includes excursions and entertainment.

Table 3.5: Lao PDR International Tourist Arrivals, Tourism Receipts, and Receipts per International Tourist, 2014–2019

($ million)

Year	International Tourist Arrivals (million)	International Tourism Receipts ($ million)	Receipts per International Tourist ($)
2014	4.2	641.6	154.3
2015	4.7	725.4	154.8
2016	4.2	724.2	170.8
2017	3.9	648.1	167.5
2018	4.2	811.0	193.7
2019	4.8	934.7	195.1

Source: Author's estimates derived from MICT (2020).

Although long- and medium-haul international tourists comprise only 13.2% of total international arrivals, these markets accounted for 44.9% of total tourist spending in 2019. Their average length of stay is 8 days and average spending is $83.6 per day, generating $663.3 average expenditure per visit. In comparison, intraregional tourists typically stay 1–3 days and spend $12–$80 per day. MICT reports that Chinese tourists spend $202.6 per visit, Vietnamese $87.5, and Thai $103.7. Further segmentation indicates the combined 3.1 million Chinese, Thai, and Vietnamese tourists that entered the Lao PDR with a passport in 2019 stayed 3-times longer and spent more than twice as much per day than intraregional tourists from these markets that enter with a border pass.[17] The importance of attracting higher-spending segments of these three intraregional markets to boost tourism receipts should not be overlooked, especially considering the average spending per international trip by Chinese tourists worldwide is estimated to be $2,000 (McKinsey & Company 2018).

Table 3.6 illustrates the Lao PDR's high intensity of tourism services and tourist arrival patterns discussed above. Tourism services are predominately provided by Lao-owned private enterprises (92%). The few large foreign-owned international hotels and travel agencies are mainly found in Vientiane Capital, Vientiane Province, and Louangphabang. Bokeo, Savannakhet, and Vientiane Province each have one foreign-owned casino-hotel with about 500 rooms each.

Table 3.6: Lao PDR Tourism Services and Tourist Arrivals by Province, 2019

| Province | Accommodations | | | Tour Operators | | International Tourists | | Domestic Tourists | |
	Rooms	Share (%)	Occupancy (%)	Number	Share (%)	Number	Share (%)	Number	Share (%)
Attapu	823	1.5	54	3	0.6	164,139	2.2	66,793	2.8
Bokeo	1,412	2.5	67	15	2.8	637,842	8.7	52,442	2.2
Bolikhamxai	2,913	5.2	47	6	1.1	157,607	2.1	134,169	5.7
Champasak	3,793	6.8	49	27	5.0	1,077,645	14.6	292,093	12.4
Houaphan	984	1.8	40	2	0.4	58,757	0.8	23,401	1.0
Khammouan	2,286	4.1	57	6	1.1	444,396	6.0	149,078	6.3
Louang-Namtha	1,509	2.7	64	7	1.3	661,852	9.0	40,549	1.7
Louangphabang	6,746	12.1	69	81	15.0	638,101	8.7	221,934	9.4
Oudomxai	2,231	4.0	65	5	0.9	118,468	1.6	112,118	4.8
Phongsali	915	1.6	47	2	0.4	160,012	2.2	8,623	0.4
Salavan	816	1.5	52	2	0.4	112,770	1.5	82,450	3.5
Savannakhet	4,686	8.4	53	10	1.9	650,339	8.8	476,697	20.3
Xekong	706	1.3	51	0	0.0	55,438	0.8	53,559	2.3
Vientiane Capital	14,013	25.2	59	317	58.8	1,868,985	25.4	144,232	6.1
Vientiane Province	6,372	11.5	61	32	5.9	329,857	4.5	382,139	16.3
Xaisomboun	336	0.6	46	0	0.0	21,252	0.3	17,465	0.7
Xaignabouli	2,557	4.6	41	16	3.0	117,172	1.6	29,222	1.2
Xiangkhouang	2,443	4.4	51	8	1.5	83,407	1.1	63,887	2.7
Total	**55,541**	**100.0**	**54**	**539**	**100.0**	**7,358,039**	**100.0**	**2,350,851**	**100.0**

Lao PDR = Lao People's Democratic Republic.
Source: MICT (2019 and 2020).

---

[17] 1.0 million intraregional tourists from the PRC, Thailand, and Viet Nam entered with a border pass in 2019.

The number of accommodations businesses increased 20.4% during 2014–2019 (Table 3.7). While the number of hotels rose steadily each year, 2016 saw guesthouse openings sharply increase following the 12.6% surge in international arrivals in 2015. The subsequent 10.0% decrease in arrivals in 2016—partly affected by fewer tourists from Thailand which encouraged local tourism through tax incentives in 2016–2017—led to 11.7% fewer guesthouses and 20.5% fewer restaurants in 2017. Guesthouse and restaurant openings each rebounded about 12% in 2018.

Table 3.7: Lao PDR Tourism Service Enterprises, 2014–2019
(number and % growth)

	2014	2015	2016	2017	2018	2019	Change 2014–2019 (%)
Accommodations	2,426	2,449	2,997	2,734	3,102	2,920	20.4
Hotel	515	542	545	569	670	637	23.7
Guesthouse[a]	1,911	1,907	2,452	2,165	2,432	2,283	19.5
Total rooms	44,714	48,386	46,513	50.600	56,825	55,541	24.2
Occupancy rate	54.0%	57.0%	51.0%	54.0%	53.0%	54.0%	0.0
Restaurant	1,269	1,664	2,969	2,360	2,646	2,679	111.1
Entertainment	164	164	365	249	305	246	50.0
Travel Agent	342	368	381	422	503	539	57.6

Lao PDR = Lao People's Democratic Republic.
[a] Includes resorts.
Source: Ministry of Information, Culture and Tourism. Annual Statistical Reports on Tourism in Laos (Years: 2014–2019).

The Lao PDR's accommodations subsector is characterized by small family-run hotels and guesthouses with varying service quality. In 2019, the average number of bedrooms in the hotel category is 39, while guesthouses and resorts average 13 bedrooms. In the same year, provincial occupancy rates ranged from 40% in Houaphan to 69% in Louangphabang. Excess inventory and low average daily rates undermine revenue per available room, a key accommodations performance metric.[18] For example, given international tourists spent an estimated $202.7 million on accommodations in 2018 (25% of total receipts) and the national room inventory totaled 56,825, revenue per available room was about $14. In comparison, average revenue per available room in Southeast Asia was $82.5 based on 70.2% average occupancy and $117.4 average daily rate.

---

[18] Daily rates typically range $15–$35 for guesthouses and $40–$120 for hotels.

Louangphabang has seven luxury hotels with a total of 314 bedrooms. In 2018, the average daily rate for this segment was $293; however, 33.5% occupancy generated only $98 per available room (Horwath HTL 2019). Still, revenue per available room was 19% higher than Southeast Asia's average, demonstrating that the Lao PDR can provide the quality accommodation services needed to attract high-spending markets. Louangphabang has one additional luxury hotel in its development pipeline which will add 54 bedrooms to this category when it opens in 2022. Louangphabang's upscale category, with rooms typically priced $120–$200 per night, comprises 16 properties with about 400 bedrooms. There are two upscale hotels in the development pipeline expected to add 174 additional rooms in 2021.

Tourism Employment

The Lao PDR's comprehensive 2018 tourism and hospitality enterprise survey estimated that tourism directly sustains 54,400 jobs, including travel, accommodations, and retail enterprises (Ministry of Education and Sports 2018). The in-depth survey assessed 1,270 businesses with 42,600 workers and found that the handicraft and accommodations subsectors generate the most jobs (Table 3.8). Women hold more jobs than men and nearly 9% of workers are from vulnerable groups. The Ministry of Education and Sports estimates that 2,000 tourism and hospitality graduates enter the workforce each year, indicating labor supply is adequate for the near term. However, the percentage of incumbent Lao workers that hold a tourism-related qualification is only 3.1%. The proportion that received any type of formal training is 12.6%, with the balance lacking the basic literacy, numeracy, and problem-solving skills needed to perform effectively. Handicraft production, performing arts, and tour guiding, which require specialized technical skills or foreign language aptitude, are the hardest occupational vacancies to fill.

Foreign workers are employed mainly as managers of luxury and upscale hotels and resorts, and by international tour operators. Relatively high percentages of foreign restaurant employees reflect the wide availability of quality international cuisine, particularly in Vientiane Capital and Louangphabang. According to the Lao PDR's Labor Law (Government of the Lao PDR 2013), employers must prioritize hiring Lao nationals, with quotas for foreign workers approved each year by the Ministry of Labor and Social Welfare. The ratio of foreign to Lao employees is capped at 15% for foreigners working as broadly defined manual laborers and 25% for technical experts/managers. The Lao Tourism Law (Government of the Lao PDR 2013) prohibits foreigners from working as tour guides, but 100% foreign ownership of hotels, resorts, and restaurants is permitted. Tour companies may be up to 80% foreign owned.

Table 3.8: Lao PDR Tourism Employment Characteristics by Subsector, 2018

Subsector	Jobs	Share of Tourism Employment (%)	Women (%)	Temporary Workers (%)	Foreign Workers (%)	Vulnerable Workers (%)	Vacancies
Hotel	8,564	20.3	56.1	1.2	5.0	3.0	183
Resort	2,203	5.2	55.2	2.3	3.5	10.9	39
Guesthouse	2,841	6.7	59.7	0.2	1.2	5.6	50
Restaurant	4,526	10.7	59.4	7.1	4.2	3.9	47
Entertainment	3,594	8.5	41.8	1.7	0.4	1.5	52
Travel services	1,389	3.3	26.4	14.9	2.6	8.1	61
Tourist attraction	4,728	11.2	45.0	2.2	0.3	6.3	201
Handicrafts	14,435	34.2	83.4	0.9	0.5	16.3	707
Total	**42,260**	**100.0**	**62.5**	**2.3**	**2.0**	**8.6**	**1,399**

Lao PDR = Lao People's Democratic Republic.
Notes: Workers categorized as vulnerable met at least one of the following criteria: member of a poor household; live in rural/remote area; lack basic education; ethnic minority; orphan, survivor of human trafficking, sexual crimes or violence; disabled, affected by chronic illness, or recovering from drug addiction. Resorts and handicraft production tend to be in rural areas, explaining the high percentage of vulnerable workers in these subsectors.
Source: Ministry of Education and Sports (2018).

Use of Information Technology

Information technology is used in the Lao PDR to market tourism services, provide visitor information, and support a range of administrative functions. Common consumer touch points include search engines and websites to gather destination information; online travel agents to book transport, accommodations, and tours; and social media for sharing experiences. Larger hotels and tour operators use digital tools and services for direct marketing, to automate and make business processes more efficient, and to improve customer experiences. However, few small and medium-sized tourism enterprises effectively use digital services because of low awareness and relatively high broadband costs. Although the Lao PDR's mobile phone ownership is around 87%, the subscription rate for mobile broadband internet is only 35%, and around 3% for fixed broadband service (World Bank 2018b).

Before COVID-19, global demand for online travel services was set to grow from $570 billion in 2017 to $1.1 trillion in 2023 (Market Watch 2020). Despite this opportunity, the Lao PDR lists fewer than 550 tours on Tripadvisor, much lower than Cambodia's 3,475 listed tours.[19] Lao businesses' use of other online

---

[19] See Tripadvisor. Laos: Tours and Tickets. https://www.tripadvisor.com/Attraction_Products-g293949-Laos.html (accessed 14 July 2020).

resources such as Alibaba, AirBnB, and Expedia are also typically lower than regional comparators. As both domestic and international tourists use information technology to research and purchase tourism services, more Lao businesses should take advantage of the cost-effective marketing opportunities they provide. Chinese travelers are particularly inclined to use digital booking platforms and mobile applications to pay for services and goods. Businesses that offer Alipay and WeChat Pay payment options can significantly boost revenues, especially from the 43% of younger Chinese travelers that prefer paying with mobile devices (McKinsey & Company 2018).

Conclusion

The onset of COVID-19 has paralyzed the tourism sector worldwide as countries closed their borders. The UNWTO suggested that international arrivals worldwide could decline by up to 78% in 2020 (UNWTO 2020a). International arrivals in the Lao PDR plummeted by 81.5% in 2020 compared with 2019 (Vientiane Times 2021b). Despite the tourism downturn in 2020, the Lao PDR has several strengths that can help its tourism industry quickly recover once international borders reopen to tourists. These include its strategic location in the center of populous Southeast Asia, with nearby markets showing a strong and growing affinity for the types of culture and nature-based tourism the country offers. Good gateway airports and transnational roads ease international access, as do open visa policies for select markets. Importantly, the Lao people's reputation for offering gracious hospitality in safe, relaxed, and uncrowded natural settings are advantages that are difficult to match.

Alongside these strengths the Lao PDR should continue to improve secondary destination infrastructure and harness opportunities to use information technology to cost-effectively improve destination marketing, provide online training, and promote electronic commerce.

In the next chapter, complementarities between the agriculture and tourism sectors are examined to identify opportunities to strengthen linkages so that the expansion of tourism services benefit not only those directly employed in the tourism sector but create spillover effects for the rest of the economy.

CHAPTER 4

Exploring Linkages between Tourism and Agriculture in the Lao PDR

Manisha Pradhananga and Takashi Yamano

Introduction

The potential of tourism as a tool for growth and poverty alleviation has been recognized. The United Nations (UN) emphasized its importance by declaring 2017 as the International Year of Sustainable Tourism for Development. Tourism services are dynamic, crosscutting several sectors and hence likely to stimulate productivity in various sectors of the economy. Tourism contributes significantly to gross domestic product (GDP), exports, and foreign exchange earnings in many developing countries, where other sectors are underdeveloped. Generally labor-intensive with low barriers to entry, tourism services can provide opportunities for local residents, including women and other disadvantaged groups, to generate income and participate in decent work.[20]

However, the benefits to be gained from tourism are not automatic, but are contingent on the quality of jobs created and the strength of linkages between tourism and the rest of the economy. Furthermore, tourism can bring adverse environmental, distributional, and cultural effects. If poorly managed, tourism growth can bring about pollution of local land and water resources and damage biodiversity and the environment. The industry can be resource-intensive and diminish access to valuable community resources. Tourism can also have negative cultural effects leading to increase in crime

---

[20] The International Labour Organization (ILO) defines decent work as work that is productive and that delivers a fair income; workplace security and social protection for families; better prospects for personal development and social integration; freedom for people to express their concerns, organize, and participate in decisions that affect their lives; and equality of opportunity and treatment for all women and men. ILO. Decent Work. https://www.ilo.org/global/topics/decent-work/lang--en/index.htm.

and sexual exploitation. To ensure that tourism benefits the economy, the government must develop strong linkages between tourism and other economic sectors, and put in place proper management measures to ensure that sustainable growth benefits the local population.

So far, growth in the Lao PDR has not been inclusive. Inequality has increased even as absolute poverty declined. As discussed in Chapter 1, one reason for the rise in inequality is the overreliance on capital-intensive natural resources such as mining and hydropower, which has created limited opportunities for gainful employment. The tourism sector can benefit the Lao economy by expanding markets for agriculture and handicraft products, and by providing job opportunities especially in remote locations.

The ADB country diagnostic study for the Lao PDR (ADB 2017a) identified the considerable potential of the agriculture and tourism sectors in promoting inclusive growth. Chapter 1 of the report presented and discussed the framework based on the AGRO Matrix, while Chapter 2 explained possible linkages of agriculture with other sectors. This chapter will then explore the direct interlinkages and complementarities between these two sectors.

ADB performed two rounds of tourism enterprise surveys, in 2019 and 2020, covering accommodation enterprises and restaurants in four major tourism destinations in the Lao PDR: Louangphabang, Vangviang, Vientiane Capital, and Champasak. The 2019 survey presents a snapshot of the tourism sector in the Lao PDR before the COVID-19 pandemic, detailing the characteristics of tourism enterprises along with estimates of employment generated and links with the agriculture industry. The 2020 survey estimates the initial impact of COVID-19 on tourism businesses and jobs and the policy measures they favored.

Tourism Clusters in the Lao PDR

As discussed in Chapter 3, tourism in the Lao PDR has three subregional clusters: Louangphabang, Louang-Namtha, and Bokeo provinces in the north; Vientiane Capital and Vientiane Province in the center; and Khammouan, Savannakhet, and Champasak provinces in the south. The ADB surveys covered major tourism destinations in all three clusters (Figure 4.1). This section will compare tourism markets and attractions in each cluster particularly in the surveyed provinces and explore opportunities to strengthen linkages between tourism, the labor market, and agriculture.

Figure 4.1: Tourism Clusters in the Lao PDR

LAO PEOPLE'S DEMOCRATIC REPUBLIC
TOURISM CLUSTER

Northern Cluster
Central Cluster
Southern Cluster

PHONGSALI

LOUANG-NAMTHA
Louang-Namtha

BOKEO
Houayxay

Xai

LOUANGPHABANG

Xam-Nua

OUDOMXAI

HOUAPHAN

Louangphabang

XAIGNABOULI

XIANGKHOUANG
Pek

Xaignabouli

XAISOMBOUN
Anouvong

VIENTIANE
Viengkham

BOLIKHAMXAI
Pakxan

VIENTIANE

VIENTIANE
CAPITAL

KHAMMOUAN

Thakhek

Kaysone Phomvihane
SAVANNAKHET

Salavan
SALAVAN   XEKONG
Lamam

Pakxe

Samakhixai
ATTAPU

CHAMPASAK

0   50   100
Kilometers

National Capital
Provincial Capital
Provincial Boundary
International Boundary
Boundaries are not necessarily authoritative.

This map was produced by the cartography unit of the Asian Development Bank.
The boundaries, colors, denominations, and any other information shown on this
map do not imply, on the part of the Asian Development Bank, any judgment on the
legal status of any territory, or any endorsement or acceptance of such boundaries,
colors, denominations, or information.

2100010B 20LAO ABV

Source: Authors.

Clearly, each cluster attracts different types of tourists, with varying motivations for travel and service quality expectations. Louangphabang tends to attract higher-spending, independent travelers who are willing to spend more for an authentic experience. Champasak attracts the lower-spending market comprising mostly of regional package tours and backpackers. Vientiane Capital attracts all markets, with a higher proportion of business travelers lifting overall tourist spending. Recently, Vangviang has been able to attract higher-spending international and domestic tourists.

Northern Cluster: Louangphabang

Louangphabang province in the northern part of the Lao PDR is a well-established tourist destination. It has 224 cultural, natural, and historic tourism sites, including the town of Louangphabang, a United Nations Educational, Scientific and Cultural Organization (UNESCO) World Heritage site. Besides its many handicraft villages, the province offers river cruises, agritourism, and trekking, which appeal to diverse markets.

Louangphabang's international airport serves direct flights from Thailand (Bangkok, Chiang Mai), Viet Nam (Ha Noi), Cambodia (Siem Reap), the People's Republic of China (PRC) (Chengdu, Jinghong), and Singapore as well as domestic flights connecting to Vientiane Capital and Champasak. The nearest international land border crossings are in Chiang Khong, Thailand, and Mohan, PRC. Route 13 links the province to Vangviang and Vientiane Capital. About 58% of visitors arrive through Louangphabang airport, 34.8% enter by land, and 7.2% arrive by boat.

In 2019, Louangphabang received about 638,000 international visitors and 222,000 domestic tourists. Only 5.5% of total visitors in the country are long-haul tourists from Europe and the Americas, but they make up over 42% of all visitors to Louangphabang. Tourists from the Association of Southeast Asian Nations (ASEAN) and Asia and the Pacific make up over 94% of arrivals, while these tourists comprise about 57% of arrivals in Louangphabang (Table 4.1).

Table 4.1: Composition of Tourist Arrivals[a] by Region, 2019
(%)

	ASEAN	Asia and the Pacific	Europe	Americas	Africa and Middle East
Lao PDR	66.8	27.5	3.8	1.7	0.2
Louangphabang	23.7	33.4	28.3	13.8	0.9
Vientiane Capital	72.6	22.3	3.1	1.8	0.2
Champasak	87.1	4.4	6.3	1.8	0.3

ASEAN = Association of Southeast Asian Nations, Lao PDR = Lao People's Democratic Republic.
[a]Based on port of entry.
Source: MICT (2019).

Over of 65% visitors to Louangphabang are independent travelers. Although independent traveling guests from Europe and the Americas tend to stay longer, they spend less per day compared with those taking prearranged tours. Asian visitors tend to be consumers of middle-market to upmarket package tours (UNCTAD 2014). Table 4.2 shows that visitors from the PRC to the Lao PDR increased four times between 2013 and 2019, largely as a result of the trade and tourism cooperation between the two countries, coupled with the rise of the Chinese middle class who now travel abroad. The number of Chinese visitors is expected to increase even more when the Lao PDR–PRC railway begins operating in 2021. Louangphabang also witnessed a big jump in the number of tourists from Thailand between 2013 and 2019. It is not surprising that Louangphabang has the highest room occupancy rate (70%) among the four areas.

Table 4.2: Number of Visitors to Louangphabang, Top 10 Nationalities, 2013 and 2019

	2013	2019
Domestic	125,354	221,934
PRC	20,802	90,567
Thailand	41,725	77,892
Republic of Korea	14,683	38,531
United Kingdom	29,051	35,007
United States	26,243	57,020
France	27,766	33,592
Germany	26,229	32,561
Canada	17,824	25,973
Japan	15,132	19,312
Australia	16,817	19,301

PRC = People's Republic of China.
Source: MICT (2019).

Central Cluster: Vangviang and Vientiane Capital

Vangviang

Vangviang is a small town in Vientiane Province, strategically located midway between Vientiane Capital and Louangphabang on Road No. 13 North, the country's main north–south transport artery also connected to Vientiane Capital by a new expressway that has reduced driving time between destinations to about 1 hour. Formerly a low-budget backpacker destination, Vangviang has recently reinvented itself as a family-friendly nature and adventure destination attracting high-spending tourists (Surana 2016). Visitors enjoy the attractive limestone formations set against the Nam Song River and rural landscapes. Nature and adventure-based activities such as kayaking, rock climbing, hiking, ziplining, and exploring caves are also popular among visitors.

In 2018, more than 1 million international tourists visited Vangviang. The Republic of Korea became one of Vangviang's top markets beginning in 2015 after a popular Korean television program was filmed in the area. Visitors from the Republic of Korea are now the third largest group of foreign tourists in the country. Vangviang has also emerged as a destination for domestic tourists— between 2014 and 2018 domestic tourist arrivals increased by almost three times to 357,800.

Vientiane Capital

As the economic center of the Lao PDR, Vientiane Capital hosts commercial establishments, government offices, international organizations, and several iconic attractions among its 84 cultural, natural, and historic tourist sites. Vientiane Capital has the country's largest and busiest international airport, with scheduled flights connecting to Bangkok, Chiang Mai, Ha Noi, Ho Chi Minh City, Kuala Lumpur, Kunming, Phnom Penh, Siem Reap, Seoul, Singapore, Guangzhou, Changsha, and Busan. The Lao–Thai Friendship Bridge connects the capital to Thailand.

Vientiane Capital is the Lao PDR's most industrialized city, in 2019 recording the highest number of international arrivals at close to 1.9 million. About two-thirds of arrivals in Vientiane Capital are short-haul tourists from ASEAN countries; and about 19% are from the Asia and Pacific region. Vientiane Capital is also the country's top domestic tourist destination, hosting more than 700,000 domestic visitors, or 25% of total domestic trips in 2018.

Southern Cluster: Champasak

Champasak province is in the southwest part of the country, bordering Cambodia and Thailand. Major attractions in Champasak include the Vat Phou and Associated Ancient Settlements within the Champasak Cultural Landscape, a UNESCO World Heritage site, and the Khone Phapheng waterfall at Siphandone (4,000 Mekong River islands). Champasak's Bolaven Plateau with its rich volcanic soil and cool climate is an emerging agritourism destination.

Champasak's international tourist arrivals increased from 535,419 in 2014 to 1,077,645 in 2019. Champasak attracts mainly Thai tourists, who made up more than 80% of international arrivals in 2018. Thai visitors on package tours tend to stay for 3 days and spend about $50 per day. Most long-haul European, North American, and Australian visitors are independent travelers who spend around $68–$123 per day and stay in Champasak for 5–6 days while on a longer visit to the country.

Champasak's Pakxe International Airport, only 5 kilometers (km) from Pakxe city center, has direct international connections to Siem Reap, Phnom Penh, and Bangkok, and domestic connections to Vientiane Capital, Louangphabang, and Savannakhet. The Vang Tao border-crossing with Thailand is an important port of entry into Champasak. In 2019, Pakxe International Airport welcomed 12,545 tourists to the country, while 184,863 tourists entered through the Van Tao border and 18,429 tourists crossed the Nong Nok Khien border from Cambodia.

ADB Tourism Enterprise Surveys (2019 and 2020): Survey Design

ADB carried out two rounds of tourism enterprise surveys in the Lao PDR, the first one in 2019 and a follow-up in 2020. The surveys closely followed the methodology of the Tourism and Hospitality Enterprise Survey of Employment and Skills in Lao PDR (ESS), which was performed in early 2018. The ESS is the most comprehensive survey in the tourism and hospitality sector in the country covering 17 provinces and the Vientiane Capital (Ministry of Education and Sports 2018). It included restaurants and enterprises providing accommodation (hotels, resorts, guesthouses), entertainment, travel services, and handicrafts. While the ADB surveys focused on accommodation and restaurants in four locations— Louangphabang province, Vangviang district, Vientiane Capital, and Champasak province—they covered all registered establishments employing six or more persons in the resort, hotel, and restaurant subsectors; and those employing three or more persons in the guesthouse subsector.

For the face-to-face interviews conducted from 4 July to 2 August 2019, a team of four enumerators and two supervisors were recruited. Of the 408 relevant enterprises covered by the ESS, the team was able to interview 366 enterprises.[21] Table 4.3 provides a breakdown of enterprises by subsector and location.

---

[21] Of the 408 relevant enterprises included in the ESS, 34 were found to be closed between 2018 and 2019, while 8 refused to be surveyed.

Table 4.3: Number of Enterprises Surveyed, 2019 and 2020

	Louangphabang	Vangviang	Vientiane Capital	Champasak	Total
2019 Survey					
Hotel	36	15	85	33	169
Resort	11	8	9	8	36
Guesthouse	14	3	69	17	103
Restaurant	15	9	27	7	58
Total	**76**	**35**	**190**	**65**	**366**
2020 Survey					
Hotel	32	15	72	31	150
Resort	9	8	9	5	31
Guesthouse	10	3	69	16	98
Restaurant	13	9	19	7	48
Total	**64**	**35**	**169**	**59**	**327**

Source: Authors' calculations based on survey data.

To assess the impact of COVID-19 on tourism enterprises, ADB conducted a follow-up survey in 2020 using an online questionnaire through operator-assisted phone interviews. The interviews were carried out between 6 May and 22 May 2020. Six interviewers, four of whom were involved in the 2019 survey, were mobilized. Of the 366 enterprises interviewed in 2019, repeat interviews were conducted on 89.3% or 327 enterprises.

2019 Survey Findings

This section provides a snapshot of tourism enterprises in the Lao PDR in 2019, before the COVID-19 pandemic. It also describes briefly the characteristics of tourism enterprises, along with the jobs generated and linkages with the agriculture industry.

Characteristics of Tourism Enterprises

Of the 366 enterprises surveyed in 2019, a majority (84%) comprised accommodation enterprises, while the remainder were restaurants. Vientiane Capital had the highest concentration of tourism enterprises at 52%, followed by Louangphabang, Champasak, and Vangviang. Among accommodation enterprises, hotels made up the majority at 55%, followed by guesthouses at 33%, while 12% were classified as resorts. The majority (55%) of enterprises are small, employing 6–20 individuals. In 2018 and 2019, 34%–36% of the hotels across the country were located in Vientiane Capital,

11%–13% in Louangphabang, 9%–10% in Champasak, and 6% in Bolikhamxai (MICT 2019).

More accommodation enterprises were star rated in 2019 than in 2018 (101 versus 89). Louangphabang now has the highest share of rated enterprises (69%) and the highest share of 4- and 5-star ratings (58%). In Vientiane Capital and Vangviang, only 23% of enterprises are rated, and in Champasak only 26% (Table 4.4).[22]

Table 4.4: Characteristics of Tourism Enterprises, 2019

Characteristics	Louangphabang	Vangviang	Vientiane Capital	Champasak	Total
Firm size[a]					
Micro	14	7	40	15	76
Small	29	18	116	41	204
Medium	32	10	30	9	81
Large	1	0	3	0	4
Very large[b]	0	0	1	0	1
Total	**76**	**35**	**190**	**65**	**366**
Accommodation rating[c]					
No star rating	19	20	125	43	207
With star rating	42	6	38	15	101
5 stars	3	0	4	0	7
4 stars	15	4	5	3	27
3 stars	23	1	24	8	56
1–2 stars	1	1	5	4	11
Total	**61**	**26**	**163**	**58**	**308**

[a]   Micro: <6 employees; small: 6–20 employees; medium: 21–100 employees; large: 101–200 employees; very large: >200 persons.
[b]   As there is only one firm that can be categorized as very large, for the rest of the chapter firms with >100 employees are categorized as large.
[c]   Among hotels, resorts, and guesthouses only.
Source: Authors' calculations based on survey data.

The ESS survey found strong correlation between firms with a web presence (websites, Facebook page, or online booking) and higher levels of capacity utilization. The ADB 2019 survey indicated that web presence is quite high for enterprises in the four locations: 42% of enterprises have a website, 32% have a Facebook page, and 44% of accommodations take online bookings from external websites such as Expedia.com, Booking.com, etc. Enterprises in Louangphabang have the strongest web presence: 46% have a Facebook page, 66% a website, and 85% accept online bookings (Table 4.5).

---

[22]   Hotels and resorts are rated by the provincial Department of Information, Culture and Tourism Office.

Table 4.5: Web Presence and Origin of Customers, 2019

Characteristics	Louangphabang	Vangviang	Vientiane Capital	Champasak	Total
Web presence (number of firms)					
Facebook page	35	13	54	17	119
Website	50	19	55	30	154
Online booking[a,b]	52	20	58	32	162
Booking method[a] (% share)					
By phone	20	23	15	15	17
Walk in	19	24	66	56	51
Direct through apps[c]	5	6	2	2	3
External booking services[b]	41	27	13	18	21
Others	15	21	4	10	9
Origin of customers (average %)					
Lao PDR (within province)	6	11	41	23	27
Lao PDR (other provinces)	11	23	20	28	20
ASEAN	16	18	15	16	16
Other Asians[d]	31	31	13	12	18
Other nationality	36	17	11	22	19

ASEAN = Association of Southeast Asian Nations, Lao PDR = Lao People's Democratic Republic, PRC = People's Republic of China.
[a]   Among hotels, resorts, and guesthouses only.
[b]   Agoda, Expedia, Booking.com, Lonely Planet, Tripadvisor, others.
[c]   Facebook, WhatsApp, WeChat, etc.
[d]   PRC, Republic of Korea, Japan, India, etc.
Source: Authors' calculations based on survey data.

It is not surprising that greater web presence is strongly correlated with larger shares of international tourists. Websites and Facebook pages help disseminate information about the enterprises to a wider international audience. Furthermore, being listed as able to accept online orders allows international travelers, especially independent travelers, to identify enterprises and easily make reservations. International customers make up 83% of the clientele in Louangphabang and 66% in Vangviang, the two locations with the strongest web presence. Louangphabang and Vangviang do especially well with online bookings: 85% of accommodation enterprises in Louangphabang and 77% in Vangviang are listed on and are capable of taking bookings from popular external booking sites. Online booking is the most popular method for making reservations in Louangphabang, accounting for an average of 41% of bookings, while walk-ins are more common in Vientiane Capital (66%) and Champasak (56%).

Employment and Skills

The ESS estimated in 2018 that the tourism and hospitality sector[23] employed 41,260 workers, with 18,114 in the accommodation and food sectors (Ministry of Education and Sports 2018). The 2019 ADB survey indicated that 12,209 workers were employed in accommodation and food enterprises in the four locations (Table 4.6), with the vast majority (75.5%) in accommodations. Over half of the jobs were generated in Vientiane Capital (which roughly corresponds to 52.6% of all enterprises), followed by Louangphabang at 24.1%, Vangviang (13.0%), and Champassak (10.1%). A majority of the workers (81.5%) were employed in small and medium-sized enterprises (SMEs).

Table 4.6: Employment by Sector, Region, and Firm Size, 2019
(weighted)

Characteristics	Louangphabang	Vangviang	Vientiane Capital	Champasak	Total
Sector					
Hotel	1,566	337	4,091	517	6,511
Resort	402	608	168	335	1,513
Guesthouse	148	96	820	130	1,194
Restaurant	833	554	1,348	257	2,992
Firm size[a]					
Micro	130	139	323	84	676
Small	648	549	2,264	664	4,125
Medium	2,007	907	2,430	491	5,835
Large	162	0	1,411	0	1,573
Total	**2,948**	**1,594**	**6,428**	**1,238**	**12,209**

[a] Micro: <6 employees; small: 6–20 employees; medium: 21–100 employees; large: >100 employees.
Source: Authors' calculations based on survey data.

Female employment is over 50% in all sectors (slightly lower at 45.8% in large enterprises) and locations; it is especially high in Vangviang at 64.8% (Table 4.7). A majority of workers are Lao nationals. About 5.0% of workers in resorts are foreign nationals; 4.9% of foreign workers are in Louangphabang and mostly in large enterprises (3.5%). The majority of workers are from the same town or district. A notable exception is Vientiane Capital, with 33.5% of workers from outside the province. Large enterprises also tend to hire workers from outside the province to supplement local labor supply. More than 90% of workers are permanent, while temporary workers account for a slightly higher share in Vangviang (8.6%) and in restaurants (5.1%).

---

[23] The tourism and hospitality sector in the ESS study included the entertainment, travel services, attraction, and handicrafts, besides the accommodation and restaurant sectors.

Table 4.7: Workforce Composition, 2019
(%)

Characteristics	Female	Foreign	Disadvantaged / Disabled	Same Town or District	Same Province	Outside Province	Temporary
Sector							
Hotel	52.6	2.8	2.4	59.5	17.2	20.5	1.7
Resort	54.8	5.0	6.3	73.8	11.9	9.4	2.4
Guesthouse	56.3	1.2	7.1	63.3	9.8	25.6	0.2
Restaurant	59.4	3.7	4.5	44.6	26.8	24.9	5.1
Location							
Louangphabang	53.1	4.9	1.2	70.1	16.9	8.2	1.7
Vangviang	64.8	1.6	4.6	74.7	17.3	6.4	8.6
Vientiane Capital	52.6	2.4	4.8	46.3	17.7	33.5	1.2
Champasak	56.1	2.8	4.2	74.2	16.6	6.4	2.2
Firm size[a]							
Micro	54.4	2.5	5.9	78.1	1.9	17.5	0.6
Small	58.9	3.1	5.5	60.2	18.3	18.4	0.8
Medium	53.5	3.0	3.2	60.9	18.3	17.8	3.8
Large	45.8	3.5	0.0	43.1	17.0	36.4	0.0
Total	**54.3**	**3.1**	**3.7**	**59.2**	**17.3**	**20.4**	**2.2**

[a] Micro: <6 employees; small: 6–20 employees; medium: 21–100 persons; large: >100 employees.
Source: Authors' calculations based on survey data.

Labor turnover is a good indicator of overall morale and job satisfaction of workers. Low labor turnover helps a company maintain productivity, given the costs associated with recruiting, hiring, and training new employees. The ADB 2019 survey found that labor turnover is highest among guesthouses and restaurants, and in micro and large enterprises.

Although the tourism sector employs many occupations (accountants, gardeners, etc.) the qualifications and skills required in such occupations are not unique to the tourism and hospitality sector. The ASEAN Mutual Recognition Arrangement on Tourism Professionals identifies 32 discrete job titles under six labor divisions as core to the tourism and hospitality sector (ASEAN 2013). In the hotel services sector (accommodation and food and beverage), labor divisions include occupations in the front office, housekeeping, food production, and food and beverage service. The 2019 survey included questions related to recruitment and training for six tourism characteristic occupations identified in the ESS as occupations with the highest employment share in the accommodation and restaurant sectors. The corresponding International Standard Classification of Occupations for each occupational category are listed in Table 4.8.

Table 4.8: Tourism Occupations and ISCO-08 Codes

Occupation	4-Digit ISCO-08
Chef	3434
Kitchen helper	9412
Wait staff	5131
Housekeeping staff	5151
Front desk staff	4224
Upper manager/mid-manager	1412

ISCO = International Standard Classification of Occupations.
Source: International Labour Organization. https://www.ilo.org/public/english/bureau/stat/isco/ (accessed November 2019).

The position of upper manager is the hardest to recruit, and this trend cuts across sectors, locations, and firm sizes. The problem is especially acute in Vangviang and Champasak where 100% and 80% of the respondents, respectively, reported difficulty recruiting for the position. Only micro firms have no difficulty recruiting upper managers, likely because they are mostly family-owned, with the proprietor also functioning as the manager. There is also a shortage of mid-managers and chefs, especially in large hotels and resorts (Table 4.9).

Table 4.9: Top Three Hard-to-Recruit Positions by Sector
(% of firms reporting difficulty)

Sector	1[a]	2	3
Hotel	Upper manager	Chef	Mid-manager
	(68.5)	(50.5)	(42.9)
Resort	Upper manager	Chef	Mid-manager
	(85.7)	(66.7)	(56.5)
Guesthouse	Upper manager	Kitchen helper	Chef
	(40.0)	(25.0)	(15.4)
Restaurant	Upper manager	Chef	Mid-manager
	(43.8)	(36.2)	(25.0)

[a] The numbers refer to rank of the position based on difficulty of recruitment.
Source: Authors' calculations based on survey data.

Tourism enterprises use both formal and informal channels to recruit staff. Only large firms seem to post formal advertisements in newspapers, while micro enterprises are more likely to use informal channels. Posting on notice boards is the most popular method, followed by asking for recommendations from existing employees. Use of social media is gaining ground especially for hiring upper managers. The lack of relevant skills is cited as the main challenge in recruitment across all job categories, locations, and sectors (Table 4.10).

Table 4.10: Recruitment Method by Position, 2019
(%)

	Recommendation of Employees	Word of Mouth	Social Media	Notice Board	Ad in Local Newspaper	Walk-In	Extended Family	Other
Chef	20.9	12.1	10.2	43.7	3.4	4.4	4.4	1.0
Kitchen helper	22.1	11.7	11.7	42.9	4.3	3.1	3.1	1.2
Wait staff	26.8	8.7	9.8	39.3	3.3	6.0	4.4	1.6
Housekeeping	26.8	15.8	4.8	34.2	1.4	5.9	10.5	0.6
Front desk staff	21.8	13.2	8.9	35.8	2.3	4.9	12.3	0.9
Mid-manager	23.6	5.6	10.3	30.9	2.6	2.1	23.6	1.3
Upper manager	9.0	11.2	28.1	22.5	6.7	3.4	9.0	10.1
Total	**23.0**	**11.7**	**9.8**	**36.1**	**2.9**	**4.5**	**10.5**	**1.5**

Source: Authors' calculations based on survey data.

More than 46% of workers employed in the accommodation and restaurant sectors during the 2019 survey stated having received some form of training from their employers in 2018 (Table 4.11). On-the-job training is the most common training method across all sectors, locations, and firm sizes. In-house training by their own team is also popular among medium-sized (44.6%) and large enterprises (100%). Louangphabang stands out with the highest share of workers trained at 60.6%, ahead by a large margin over Vientiane Capital at 43.8%, Champasak at 34.8%, and Vangviang at 29.0%. In almost all job categories, medium-sized and large firms provide more training than micro and small enterprises. Overall, training tends to focus on lower-skilled jobs such as kitchen helper, wait staff, housekeeping, and front desk staff rather than on higher-skilled categories such as mid-managers and upper managers (Table 4.12).

Table 4.11: Training and Skills Development, 2019
(%)

	Workers Trained	Female Workers Trained	On-the-Job	In-House Course (Own Team)	In-House Course (External Trainer)	External Training	Labor Turnover Rate
				Training Methods Used[a]			
Sector							
Hotel	46.3	48.2	86.2	37.7	17.4	31.2	19.6
Resort	45.2	43.5	89.3	25.0	17.9	21.4	17.9
Guesthouse	42.7	44.8	93.1	17.2	0.0	27.6	22.3
Restaurant	47.4	44.8	81.6	36.7	12.2	26.5	24.3
Location							
Louangphabang	60.6	59.3	87.5	43.8	15.6	34.4	22.3
Vangviang	29.0	27.7	65.2	13.0	30.4	39.1	14.4
Vientiane Capital	43.8	45.9	90.1	29.1	5.7	23.4	20.5
Champasak	34.8	39.6	88.9	33.3	22.2	31.1	20.8
Firm size[b]							
Micro	30.0	35.1	78.4	16.2	2.7	32.4	24.4
Small	46.6	47.9	89.2	27.4	10.2	24.2	24.9
Medium	48.8	49.2	86.5	44.6	21.6	36.5	15.3
Large	39.7	36.8	100.0	100.0	40.0	20.0	27.2
Total	**46.0**	**46.7**	**87.2**	**31.9**	**12.8**	**28.6**	**20.4**

[a] Total percentage add up to greater than 100, as many enterprises use more than one method of training.
[b] Micro: <6 employees; small: 6–20 employees; medium: 21–100 employees; large >100 employees.
Source: Authors' calculations based on survey data.

Table 4.12: Training Method by Position, 2019
(%)

Position	On-the Job	In-House Course (Using Own Team)	In-House Course (Using External Training Provider)	External Training
Chef	79.4	25.7	11.4	22.9
Kitchen helper	93.1	22.1	8.3	12.4
Wait staff	94.6	20.5	9.0	9.6
Housekeeping	94.3	19.7	6.1	9.6
Front desk	86.8	21.5	7.6	14.6
Mid-manager	53.8	16.6	10.7	36.1
Upper manager	45.1	25.5	15.7	47.1
Total	**83.4**	**21.1**	**8.7**	**17.6**

Source: Authors' calculations based on survey data.

Although the overall training rate is quite high, many enterprises recognize that the training they provide to their employees is inadequate. Hotels and resorts, where the service quality expectation is higher, tend to acknowledge the insufficiency of training more than guesthouses and restaurants. Among job categories, training for upper managers is considered the least sufficient (Table 4.13).

Table 4.13: Share of Enterprises That Say the Training They Provide Is Inadequate, 2019 (%)

	Chef	Kitchen Helper	Wait Staff	Housekeeping	Front Desk	Mid-Manager	Upper Manager
Micro	11.1	0.0	16.7	12.1	10.2	20.8	0.0
Small	38.2	25.0	33.3	27.0	25.3	19.1	45.5
Medium	40.3	34.8	38.0	30.3	31.9	35.3	40.0
Large	40.0	40.0	40.0	40.0	40.0	40.0	66.7

Source: Authors' calculations based on survey data.

Linkages with the Food Sector

To understand the tourism sector's linkages with local agriculture, enterprises were asked about food expenditure and where and how they source the food. Of the surveyed accommodation enterprises, 42% serve food in their premises. About 35% of hotels serve food; more than half of the hotels in Louangphabang do so.

The average seating capacity in food-serving enterprises is 99 (Table 4.14). Enterprises in Louangphabang are smaller (about 80% of them have less than 100 seats), while more than 40% of the enterprises in the other three destinations have more than 100 seats.

To estimate the total annual food expenditure while accounting for seasonality, tourism enterprises were asked for their (i) monthly volume of customers against their capacity; and (ii) total monthly volume and prices during peak and lean months for 23 different food items including meat and fish, grains, vegetables, and fruits. From this information we then extrapolated the total annual food expenditure of tourism enterprises in the four locations.

Table 4.14: Seating Capacity of Tourism Enterprises Serving Food and Beverage by Location, 2019

	Louangphabang	Vangviang	Vientiane Capital	Champasak	Total
Average Seats					
All enterprises	71.2	120.1	106.8	111.7	99.2
Accommodation enterprises	69.0	92.3	94.8	81.2	84.1
Restaurants	75.5	153.3	121.9	194.3	123.5
Seat Capacity by Size[a] (%)					
Small	38.6	14.3	29.5	26.9	29.6
Medium	40.9	33.3	29.5	30.8	33.6
Large	20.5	52.4	41.0	42.3	36.8

[a] Small = <50 seats, medium = 50–100 seats, large = >100 seats.
Source: Authors' calculations based on survey data.

As expected, the estimated seasonality is consistent with the overall tourism arrivals, with peak season between November and February, and lean season during the rainy months from May to September (Figure 4.2). During peak months, tourism enterprises operate at 60%–80% capacity, while operation levels fall to 25%–50% during the lean season.

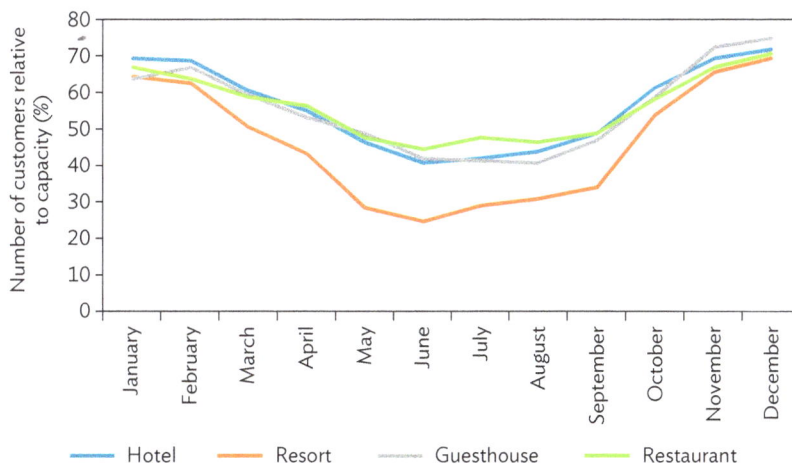

Figure 4.2: Seasonality in Tourism Enterprises, 2019

Source: Authors' calculations based on survey data.

Expenditure on meat and seafood is the largest at $4 million, and being a landlocked country, $1.19 million is spent on imported fish and seafood. Around $0.88 million is spent annually on rice and grains (Figure 4.3).

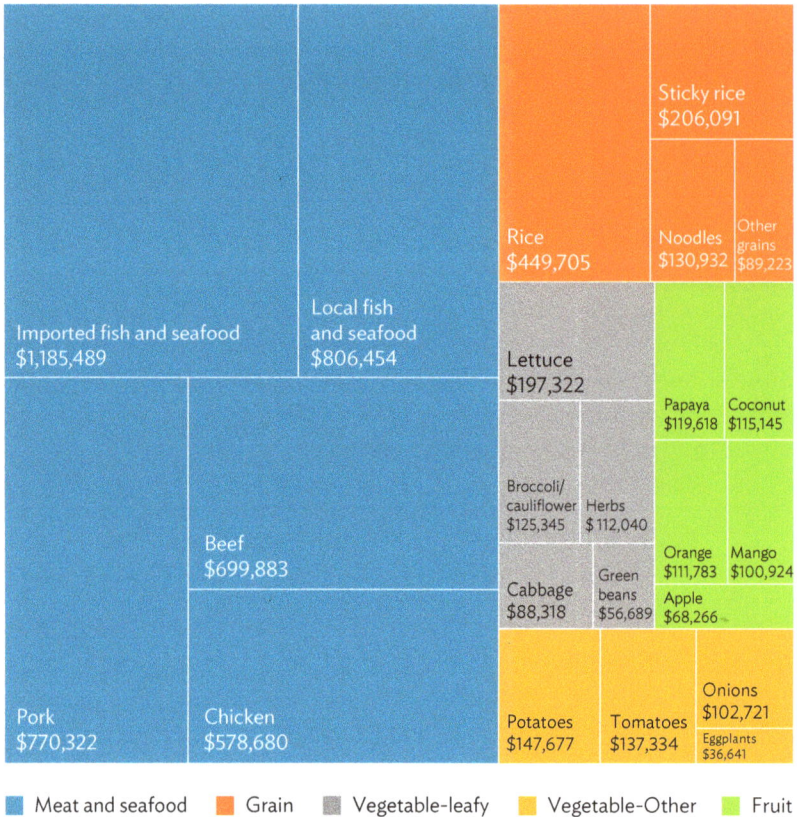

Figure 4.3: Annual Expenditure by Food Categories, 2019
($)

Imported fish and seafood $1,185,489

Local fish and seafood $806,454

Beef $699,883

Pork $770,322

Chicken $578,680

Sticky rice $206,091

Rice $449,705

Noodles $130,932

Other grains $89,223

Lettuce $197,322

Broccoli/cauliflower $125,345

Herbs $112,040

Cabbage $88,318

Green beans $56,689

Papaya $119,618

Coconut $115,145

Orange $111,783

Mango $100,924

Apple $68,266

Potatoes $147,677

Tomatoes $137,334

Onions $102,721

Eggplants $36,641

Legend: Meat and seafood · Grain · Vegetable-leafy · Vegetable-Other · Fruit

Source: Authors' calculations based on survey data.

By summing up the expenditures on the 23 major food items, the total annual food expenditure of all tourism enterprises is estimated at $6.6 million (Table 4.15), the majority of which ($4.3 million) is estimated to have been spent on Lao PDR–produced goods, while the rest ($2.3 million) was spent on imported food. As expected, total expenditure is correlated with the size of the enterprise—larger enterprises spend more money on food compared with smaller enterprises. When corrected for size by comparing expenditure per seat, small enterprises spend the most at $303 per seat compared with only $173 per seat for large enterprises. This could be due to higher meal prices or higher turnover of guests in smaller enterprises, or because larger enterprises can buy in bulk at lower prices.

Table 4.15: Annual Food Expenditure by Enterprise Size and Location, 2019 ($)

	Louangphabang	Vangviang	Vientiane Capital	Champasak	Total
Total annual expenditure[a]	2,019,307	1,788,567	2,163,694	660,618	6,632,186
Average Annual Expenditure per Enterprise					
All enterprises	21,771	21,962	17,818	12,368	18,602
Small[b]	10,147	7,585	10,690	9,076	9,921
Medium	21,326	15,050	9,969	9,335	14,440
Large	44,757	30,281	27,461	16,669	28,675
Average Annual Expenditure per Seat					
All enterprises	321.9	217.5	219.7	141.5	235.5
Small	291.8	330.5	340.6	245.5	303.4
Medium	370.7	287.6	171.7	134.7	249.7
Large	286.5	142.2	186.5	80.4	173.0

[a] Extrapolated using weights.
[b] Small = <50 seats, medium= 50–100 seats, large = >100 seats.
Source: Authors' calculations based on survey data.

Figure 4.4 shows that a majority of food items are produced in the Lao PDR. Some food produce like apples, non-rice grains, onions, and seafood are not grown, or are produced in limited quantities because of the local climatic conditions and geography. Among the four locations, Vangviang has a higher share of foreign produce, especially potatoes, onions, broccoli, and cauliflower.

The enterprises were asked how they procure food items and were presented with three choices: (i) from the local market, (ii) through contractors, or (iii) directly from farmers. On average, about 80% of the enterprises buy from the local market, 19% of enterprises use contractors, and only 2% buy directly from farmers. Larger firms tend to use contractors while smaller firms buy directly from the local market (Figure 4.5).

Of the four locations, Louangphabang enterprises get food from the local market the least at 62% and use contractors the most (32%). Only 5% purchase directly from farmers, which while low, is significantly higher than in other locations at below 1%. Over 58% of enterprises in Louangphabang buy at least one product through contractors, higher than the 38% for Vangviang,

Figure 4.4: Share of Imports in Total Food Consumption, 2019

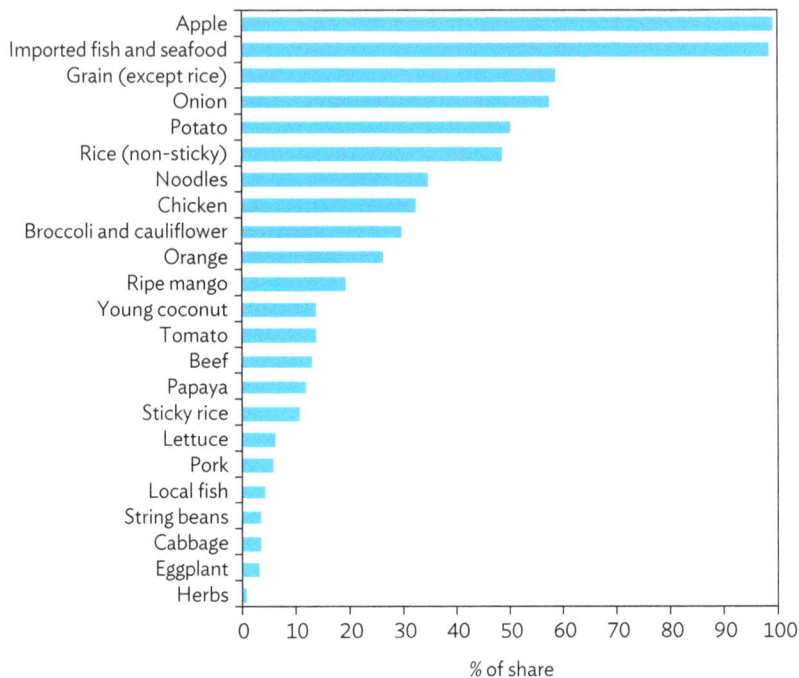

% of share

Source: Authors' calculations based on survey data.

Figure 4.5: Method of Food Purchase by Size and Location of Enterprises, 2019

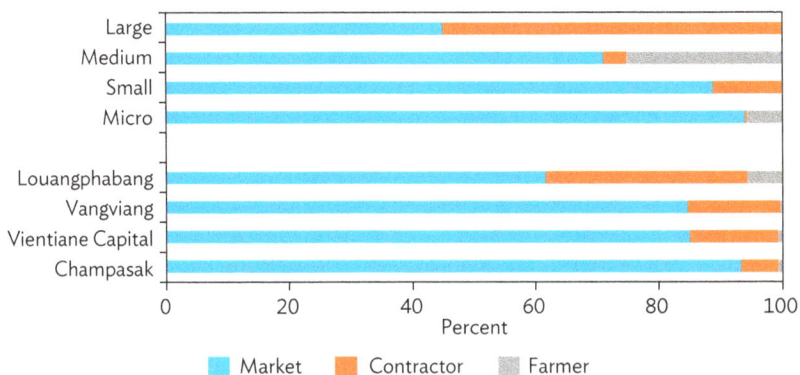

Percent

■ Market   ■ Contractor   ▨ Farmer

Source: Authors' calculations based on survey data.

30% for Vientiane Capital, and 19% for Champasak. Close to 90% of larger enterprises in Louangphabang buy from contractors. However, in Vangviang, small enterprises comprise the most (66.7%) of those that source food through contractors (Figure 4.6).

Figure 4.6: Percentage of Enterprises That Buy from Contractors, 2019

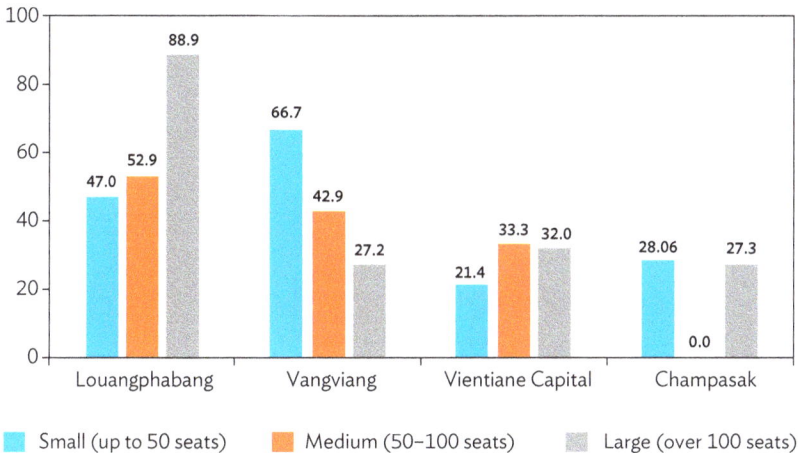

Source: Authors' calculations based on survey data.

Unlike in Louangphabang, enterprises in other locations mostly buy food items from local markets. On average, the local market is the source for about 85% of enterprises in Vientiane Capital, 83.9% in Vangviang, and 93.4% in Champasak. In Vientiane Capital and Vangviang, some food items such as meat and fish are purchased through contractors or directly from farmers. Contractors provide 20%–30% of vegetables in Vangviang, and 10%–20% in Vientiane Capital.

Overall, the demand for organic produce seems to be growing, with about 90% of enterprises indicating willingness to purchase. The interest is high in all locations, except in Champasak where only 60% of enterprises were interested in buying organic produce. More than 20% of enterprises already reported purchasing organic leafy vegetables such as lettuce, herbs, and cabbage (Table 4.16). The share is also high for vegetables such as eggplants and tomatoes, and some fruits such as papaya and oranges. Enterprises in Vientiane Capital and Louangphabang tend to purchase organic produce more than those in other locations, most likely because these locations receive more international visitors (Figure 4.7).

Table 4.16: Share of Enterprises That Purchased Organic Produce, 2019
(%)

	Did You Buy Organic?		
	Yes	No	Don't know
Lettuce	28.5	35.0	36.5
Cabbage	23.3	37.2	39.5
Broccoli/cauliflower	20.0	40.0	40.0
Coriander/parsley/mint	24.5	36.7	38.9
String beans	16.3	41.5	42.3
Tomatoes	22.1	37.2	40.7
Potatoes	7.4	42.2	50.4
Onions	6.9	43.8	49.3
Eggplants	20.8	35.4	43.8

Source: Authors' calculations based on survey data.

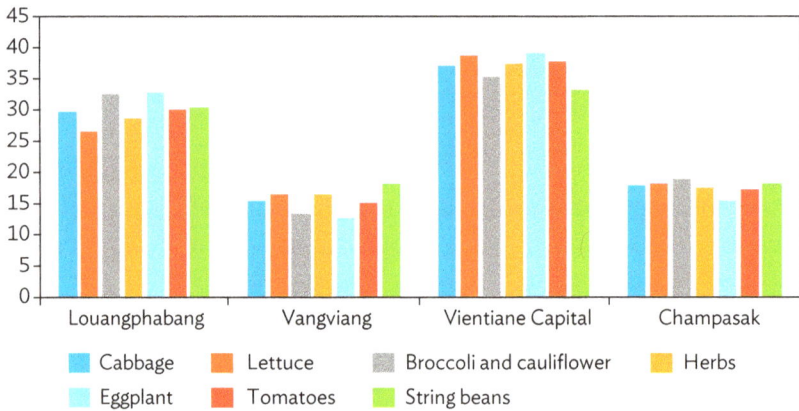

Figure 4.7: Share of Enterprises That Purchased Organic Produce by Location, 2019

Source: Authors' calculations based on survey data.

However, some 36% to over 50% of enterprises did not know if the produce they were buying were organic. This is because labeling of organic produce is still inconsistent and unreliable in the Lao PDR. Although many enterprises in Louangphabang claim to buy organic vegetables, most of the organic products are not labeled properly. In contrast, there are more organic products in Vientiane Capital that are correctly labeled.

The primary barrier to purchasing organic produce is unavailability, as reported by 55.8% of all enterprises, followed by price (24.6%), and unreliable labeling (18.4%). However, the reason varies by location: price (52%) is the topmost barrier in Vientiane Capital, unreliable labeling (53%) in Louangphabang, and unavailability in Vangviang and Champasak at 85% and 80%, respectively (Figure 4.8).

Figure 4.8: Reasons for Not Buying Organic Produce by Location, 2019
(% of respondents)

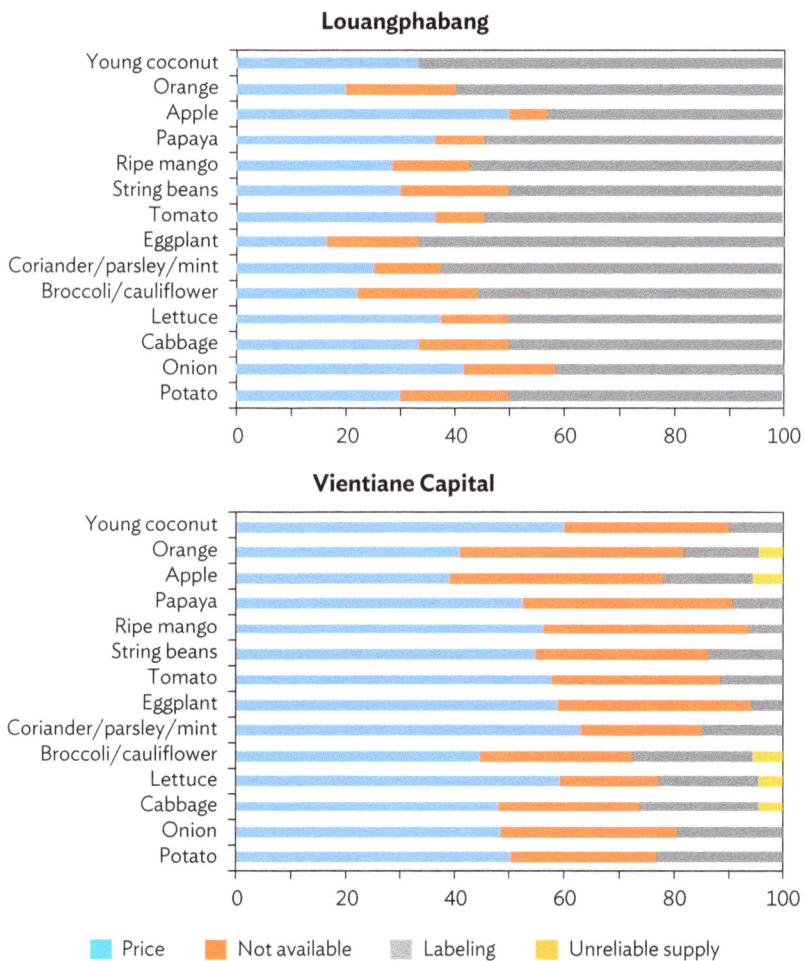

Louangphabang

Vientiane Capital

Price ■   Not available ■   Labeling ■   Unreliable supply ■

Continued next page

Figure 4.8 continued

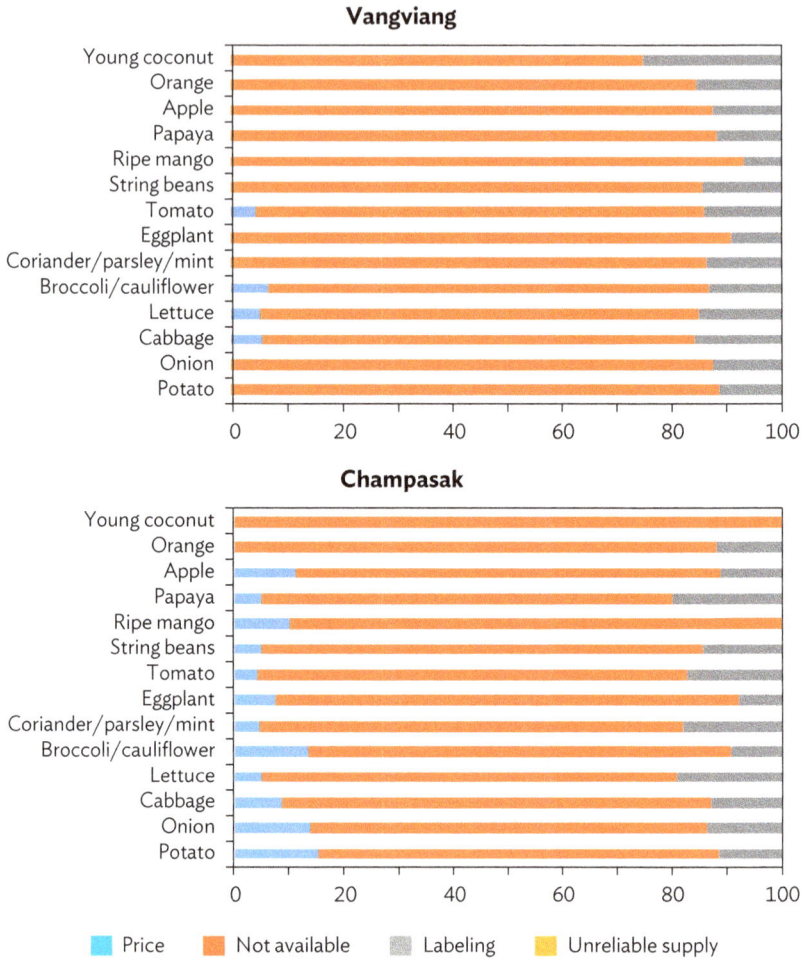

Vangviang

Champasak

Source: Authors' calculations based on survey data.

The survey data show no significant price premium for organic produce, with the exception of Louangphabang, where the price of organic vegetables is 19% higher than non-organic vegetables during peak months and 15% more during lean seasons. Although both the Lao Good Agricultural Practices (GAP) certification[24] and "Laos Organic," a third-party organic certification,[25] are

---

[24] Lao GAP is aligned with the ASEAN GAP standards.

[25] Third-party certification of organic products is mostly used for exports, with accredited bodies certifying that the products meet regulatory requirements of various markets.

available, these options may not be accessible to many small farmers because of costly bureaucratic procedures. In the past, certification and labeling were the primary concern of exporters seeking access to lucrative markets abroad. However, rising consumer awareness has seen an increasing domestic demand for safe food.[26] The survey findings confirm the growing interest in organic produce and the constraint related to unreliable and inconsistent labeling. An alternative to costly certification is a community-oriented participatory guarantee system (PGS) that employs a peer-to-peer monitoring system and is designed to meet the needs of small farmers producing for the local market. The PGS has existed in the Lao PDR since 2014 under the Department of Agriculture. Three PGS groups in Savannakhet, Xiangkhouang, and Houaphan have been certificated (ADB 2019).[27] The challenge now is to scale up and expand PGS in other locations, including in Louangphabang where labeling is identified as the most important barrier for expansion of organic produce farming and consumption.

About 59.7% of enterprises that use organic produce advertise it to their customers, and 37.8% of them claim this has boosted their business (Table 4.17). The biggest impact is seen in hotels (53.3%), enterprises in Vangviang and Champasak (both at 50.0%), and medium-sized enterprises (50.0%). By sector, resorts (72.7%); by location, Vientiane Capital (66.7%) and Vangviang (66.7%); and by firm size, the medium-sized and large enterprises (100.0%) are more likely to advertise their use of organic produce.

To summarize, the 2019 survey revealed that tourism enterprises in the four locations have strong linkages to both the domestic labor market and agriculture industry. It is estimated that in 2019 about 12,209 workers were directly employed in the food and accommodation sector in the four locations, at least half of them women. The survey also showed that tourism enterprises spend about $6.6 million on food purchases, with a majority ($4.3 million) on locally produced agriculture goods. Given the importance of tourism enterprises for both employment and its linkages with agriculture, the next section discusses the initial impact of COVID-19 on tourism enterprises.

---

[26] Safe food products are grown with controlled use of pesticides and chemical fertilizers, minimizing the risk of contamination from chemical residues or pathogens from animals or unclean water.

[27] Certification of the PGSs was supported by ADB's Core Agriculture Support Program Phase 2.

**Table 4.17: Enterprises that Advertise Use of Organic Produce
and Impact on Business, 2019** (%)

	Share of Enterprises that Advertise Use of Organic Produce[a]	Share of Enterprises with Increased Business
Sector		
Hotel	55.6	53.3
Resort	72.7	12.5
Guesthouse	66.7	0.0
Restaurant	57.1	41.7
Location		
Louangphabang	56.7	35.3
Vangviang	66.7	50.0
Vientiane Capital	66.7	35.7
Champasak	50.0	50.0
Firm Size		
Micro	50.0	0.0
Small	53.1	38.5
Medium	100.0	50.0
Large	100.0	0.0
Total	**59.7**	**37.8**

[a] Percentage share of enterprises that claim to use organic produce.
Source: Authors' calculations based on survey data.

ADB Tourism Enterprise Survey 2020: Initial Impact of COVID-19

The onset of COVID-19 has paralyzed the tourism sector worldwide as countries closed their borders, suspended commercial aviation, restricted domestic travel, and implemented quarantine measures. The United Nations World Tourism Organization (UNWTO) reported a 73% decline in international arrivals in 2020, with the largest drop of 84% in Asia and the Pacific (UNWTO 2021). Developing Asia, particularly tourism-dependent countries in Southeast Asia, fell by 82%.

The Lao PDR reported its first two COVID-19 cases on 24 March 2020.[28] A nationwide lockdown followed on 30 March 2020, prohibiting residents from leaving their homes except for essentials. All international ports of entry were closed to tourists, issuance of tourist visas was suspended, and interprovincial travel banned. International arrivals in 2020 plummeted by 81.5% compared with 2019, with arrivals dropping to zero after border closures were implemented at the end of March (Vientiane Times 2021b). Although

---

[28] Ministry of Health. COVID-19 Dashboard (in Lao). https://www.covid19.gov.la/index.php.

hotels, resorts, and restaurants were allowed to continue operating under strict guidelines, travel restrictions severely undercut visitor arrivals. In early May 2020, the Lao PDR reported only 19 confirmed COVID-19 cases and no deaths. The nationwide lockdown and intraprovincial travel restrictions were lifted starting 4 May 2020, and by 18 May 2020 tourist sites were open and interprovincial travel was permitted, including domestic flights (Savankham 2020b). However, international borders remain closed to tourists as of 1 June 2021.

However, in April 2021 the country witnessed a new outbreak of COVID-19, with cases rising to 2,356, and with 3 deaths by 7 July 2021.[29] To respond to the rise in cases, the Lao PDR government imposed preventive measures including lockdowns and domestic travel restrictions. While the Lao PDR has, thus far, avoided severe health impacts from the COVID-19 pandemic, the effect on the economy, especially the travel and tourism sector, is expected to be devastating. The Lao PDR contracted for the first time since the Asian financial crisis, as the GDP declined by 0.5% in 2020 (ADB 2021).

To assess the initial impact of COVID-19 on tourism enterprises, ADB conducted a follow-up survey from 6 May to 22 May 2020, just as restrictions on domestic travel were being loosened. Of the 366 enterprises interviewed in 2019, about 89.3% or 327 enterprises were re-interviewed. The attrition rate was relatively high in Louangphabang at 16%, most likely due to business closures. This is borne by the finding that only 22% of the Louangphabang tourism enterprises surveyed in 2019 were operating either fully or partially in May 2020 (Table 4.18). Only about 52% of enterprises surveyed in all four locations in 2019 were operating in May 2020, and this rate falls to 46% assuming the enterprises not contacted for repeat interview had closed. In Vientiane Capital, about 65% of the same enterprises were operating in May 2020, in Vangviang about 50%, and in Champasak 44%.

Relative to May 2019, 70% of tourism enterprises surveyed had reduced employees, cutting employee numbers by 38%. More female employees (40%) were laid off than male employees at 34%.[30] Even in Vientiane Capital, where many enterprises were still operational, about 65% had reduced employees. In Louangphabang and Vangviang, more than 80% had cut over 50% of their employees. The impact of COVID-19 is more severe in Louangphabang and Vangviang, where tourism enterprises mainly target international and leisure tourists, than in the other two destinations.

---

[29] A nationwide lockdown was initially announced from 30 March 2020 to 19 April 2020 under Prime Minister Order No. 06/PM (Savankham 2020a). On 15 April 2020, the lockdown was extended until 3 May 2020 (Phonevilay 2020).

[30] To account for tourism seasonality, we asked about changes in employment since May 2019.

Table 4.18: Tourism Enterprises under COVID-19 in the Lao PDR, May 2020

	Resurveyed in May 2020 (%)	Operating in May 2020 (%)	Among Resurveyed in 2020			
			Reduced Employees since May 2019[a] (%)	% Change in Employees[b]		
				All	Female	Male
Destinations	(A)	(B)	(C)	(D)	(E)	(F)
Louangphabang	84.2	21.6	82.8	(52.1)	(54.9)	(48.2)
Vangviang	100.0	50.0	82.9	(50.9)	(56.2)	(38.8)
Vientiane Capital	88.9	64.7	65.1	(33.5)	(35.4)	(29.6)
Champasak	90.8	44.2	62.7	(28.3)	(28.6)	(26.1)
Total	**89.3**	**51.6**	**70.0**	**(38.2)**	**(40.3)**	**(33.6)**

( ) = negative, Lao PDR = Lao People's Democratic Republic.
[a]   Data include all surveyed enterprises, not only those operational in May 2020.
[b]   includes temporary and permanent employees.
Source: Authors' calculations based on survey data.

About 55% of the enterprises surveyed said they have enough savings or have access to immediate credit from friends and family to remain in (or resume) business for about 5 months or until October 2020 (Table 4.19). But financial condition varies across provinces, with 55% of enterprises in Vientiane Capital reporting having enough savings to last more than 5 months, while only 48% in Louangphabang have enough savings for 4.4 months. These numbers could be underestimated because it is highly likely that the enterprises not reached for the 2020 survey are financially worse off than those able to be interviewed. About 38% of enterprises in the four regions responded that they would need to borrow money to restart their business if the tourism downturn continued beyond May 2020. More than 67% of the enterprises in Louangphabang said they would apply for the government's low-interest SME loan programs.[31]

If the pandemic continued beyond May 2020, 83% of the enterprises said they would have to temporarily close business, 56% said they would have to lay off staff, and 50% said they would have to reduce wages and salaries of their employees. Some enterprises would be forced to take drastic measures such as apply for bankruptcy (21%) or sell their business (11%) (Figure 4.9).

---

[31]   Informal discussions with members of the Lao PDR tourism industry associations suggest that while there is willingness to borrow for capital investment, there is less demand to take on debt financing to cover day-to-day operating costs and salary payments.

Table 4.19: Financial Resilience of Accommodation Enterprises by Province, May 2020

Province	Have enough savings or immediate credit (%) (A)	For how many months? (B)	Need to borrow money from financial institutions beyond May 2020 (%) (C)	Would you apply for government loan for SMEs (%) (D)
Louangphabang	48.4	4.4	43.8	67.2
Vangviang	60.0	3.6	37.1	60.0
Vientiane Capital	55.4	5.5	35.5	57.1
Champasak	55.2	5.4	36.2	53.4
Total	**54.5**	**5.0**	**37.5**	**58.8**

SMEs = small and medium-sized enterprises.
Source: Authors' calculations based on survey data.

Figure 4.9: Actions Forced to Take If COVID-19 Continues Beyond May 2020 (%)

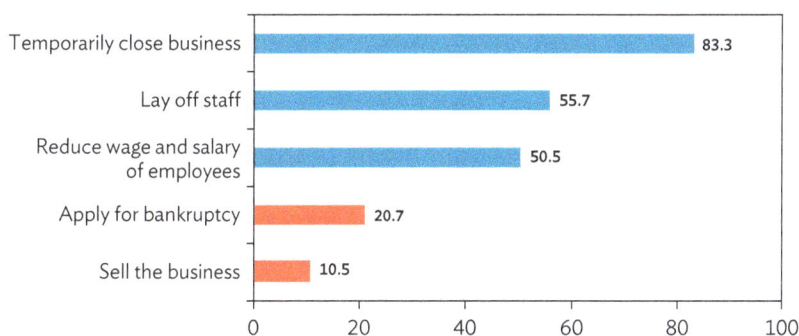

Source: Authors' calculations based on survey data.

Although 79% of respondents cite lack of working capital as a major obstacle to continuing or resuming their businesses, they are reluctant to borrow from financial institutions. As shown in Figure 4.10, the demand for special refinancing and loan repayment moratoriums is generally low at 35% and 26%, respectively. This is not surprising given the limited use of formal financial institutions for individual credit needs in the Lao PDR. Only 9% of adults (aged 15 and above) borrow from financial institutions while 31% borrow from family and friends.[32] The surveyed enterprises most favored government policy interventions in the form of tax relief (85%) and cash transfers (69%).

---

[32] World Bank. The Global Findex Database 2017. Washington, DC. https://globalfindex.worldbank.org/.

Figure 4.10: Tourism Enterprises' Approvals of Possible Government Policies, May 2020

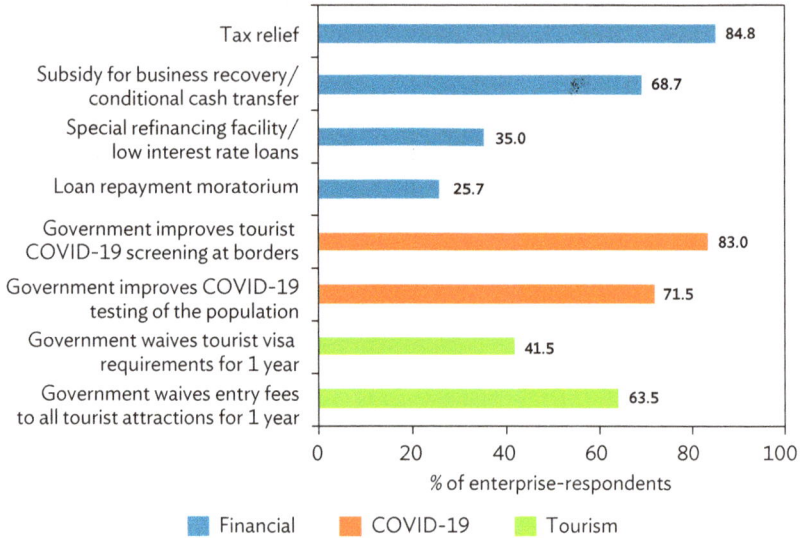

Policy	%
Tax relief	84.8
Subsidy for business recovery/ conditional cash transfer	68.7
Special refinancing facility/ low interest rate loans	35.0
Loan repayment moratorium	25.7
Government improves tourist COVID-19 screening at borders	83.0
Government improves COVID-19 testing of the population	71.5
Government waives tourist visa requirements for 1 year	41.5
Government waives entry fees to all tourist attractions for 1 year	63.5

% of enterprise-respondents

■ Financial   ■ COVID-19   ■ Tourism

Source: Authors' calculations based on survey data.

Concerns about safety and the need to rebuild consumer confidence and demand are reflected by the high percentage of respondents that strongly support improved COVID-19 screening at borders (83.0%) and improved COVID-19 testing for the general population (71.5%). Tourism-specific interventions, such as waiver of tourist visa requirements (41.5%) and entry fees to tourist attractions (63.5%), are also considered important (Figure 4.10). This view is consistent with the finding of an earlier study conducted in Macau, China in February 2020 (Fong, Law, and Ye 2020). Through a phone survey of 228 residents the study found that the respondents' outlook for the tourism industry depended on their government's ability to control the COVID-19 epidemic. They were more confident about the outlook of the tourism sector if they had a favorable view of the government's ability to control the epidemic.

As travel restrictions continue in much of the world, international travel is not expected to return to normal soon. In the meantime, domestic tourism has been put forth as a strategy to revive the sector. To assess if the magnitude of the impact varied significantly between tourism enterprises that cater primarily to domestic guests and those that are international guests oriented, the accommodation enterprises were grouped according to the proportion of domestic guests in August 2019 (Figure 4.11). The results are clear. Only about 30% of accommodation enterprises that targeted international guests remained open in May 2020;[33] while 69.4% of enterprises that targeted domestic guests did so.[34] Consequently, enterprises that primarily hosted domestic guests laid off fewer employees (26.5%) than those targeting international guests (46.3%). This indicates that enterprises catering to a larger number of domestic guests are more resilient during times of global crises, and that promoting domestic tourism should be part of the Lao PDR's post-COVID-19 recovery plan.

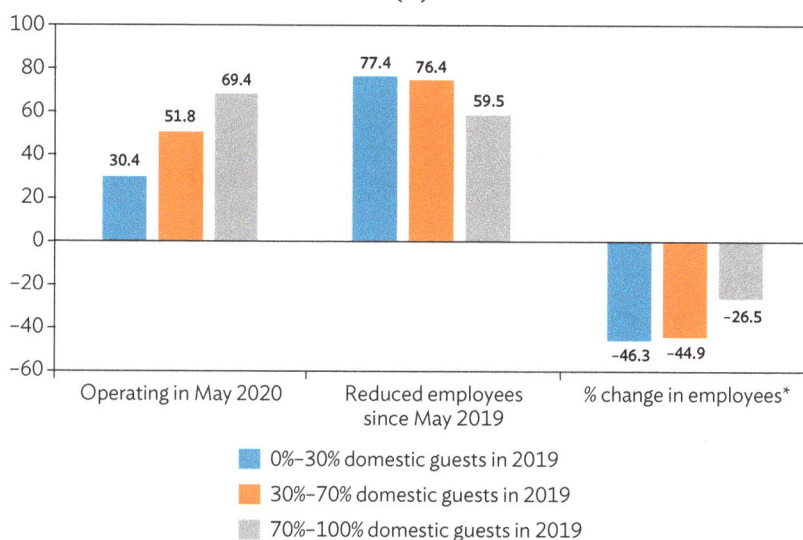

Figure 4.11: Tourism Enterprise Operation by Domestic Orientation, May 2020
(%)

* Includes temporary and permanent employees.
Source: Authors' calculations based on survey data.

Conclusion

The 2019 ADB survey of tourism enterprises in Louangphabang, Vangviang, Vientiane Capital, and Champasak revealed that the tourism sector has strong linkages to the domestic labor market and agriculture industry, which means that the locals were benefiting from the expansion of tourism services.

---

[33] Enterprises that target international guests are defined as enterprises with less than 30% domestic guests in August 2019.

[34] Enterprises that target domestic guests are defined as enterprises with more than 70% domestic guests in August 2019.

The majority of tourism enterprises are small, employing 6–20 workers. Accommodation enterprises and restaurants in the four locations employed about 12,209 workers in 2019, half of whom were women. There was an overall shortage of qualified managers, with most firms across location and size reporting difficulty in recruitment. Most tourism enterprises recognized the importance of training and skills development for their staff, to upgrade service quality. About half of the enterprises provided training opportunities for their staff, although many also recognized the inadequacy of their training.

Tourism enterprises in the four locations spent about $6.6 million per year on food, a majority of it domestically produced. Most of the food was bought from the local market, while large firms relied on contractors. The survey also showed that demand for organic fruits and vegetables is growing, with a significant share of enterprises already purchasing some organic produce. Besides unavailability, unreliable labeling and higher price discourage the purchase of organic products.

The onset of COVID-19, along with consequent restrictions for containment, is expected to have a devastating impact on the tourism sector of the Lao PDR. The ADB survey conducted in May 2020 revealed that most tourism enterprises were struggling to stay afloat; about half of the 327 tourism enterprises surveyed were temporarily closed and had reduced employees by 38%. The impact was larger for enterprises that primarily served international guests.

COVID-19 response and recovery options favored by the enterprises in the 2020 survey were consistent with UNWTO (2020) guidelines and priorities to restart tourism, which include providing businesses with liquidity and protecting jobs, recovering confidence through safety and security, and opening borders responsibly. Other preferred government interventions include tax relief and cash transfers. These policies are essential in the short and medium term to support cash flow of the enterprises so that they can stay in business. More enterprises in operation also imply fewer job cuts. Tourism enterprises also favor improved COVID-19 screening at borders and expanded testing for the population. This suggests that they are worried about increased risk of infections from domestic and foreign tourists and recognize the need to rebuild consumer confidence to travel. Finally, the importance of rolling out COVID-19 vaccines cannot be emphasized enough to control the spread of the virus and restore confidence to reopen international borders.

CHAPTER 5

Fostering Inclusive Growth in the Lao PDR: The Roles of Tourism and Agriculture

Manisha Pradhananga, Jindra Nuella Samson, Lotis Quiao, and Steven Schipani

In the last 3 decades,[35] gross domestic product (GDP) growth in the Lao People's Democratic Republic (Lao PDR) averaged a remarkable 7%, quadrupling per capita income from $445 in 1989 to $1,840 in 2019 in constant 2010 dollar terms. However, this growth was accompanied by rising inequality, with the GINI coefficient increasing from 31.0 in 1993 to 38.8 in 2019. Due to the unequal nature of growth, the Lao PDR's pace of poverty reduction was slower than other countries in the region.[36] In 2019, almost one-fifth of the population was still living under the poverty line (World Bank 2020).[37]

With nearly 90% of the poor living in rural areas, poverty is still a rural phenomenon. Lack of employment opportunities outside of agriculture is driving poverty in the country. The agriculture sector employs over 60% of the labor force, while industry, primarily driven by capital-intensive sectors, employs only 12% of the workforce and has been unable to absorb surplus labor from agriculture. The highest poverty rate is among households whose heads are unemployed (28.7%), and the majority (90%) of these household heads were previously engaged in the agriculture sector (World Bank 2020).

Given its abundant natural resources and rich cultural heritage, the Lao PDR can generate benefits for the rural population and thus lift many out of poverty by harnessing the synergies between the agriculture and tourism sectors. For instance, the government has set a goal to establish organic markets in all provinces by 2025. Tourism enterprises can be important buyers of organic

---

[35] GDP growth between 1989 to 2019 averaged 7%. World Bank. World Development Indicators. https://data.worldbank.org/products/wdi (accessed 9 January 2021).

[36] Growth elasticity of poverty for the Lao PDR is 0.71, compared with 1.33 for Viet Nam and 2.84 for Thailand.

[37] The national poverty rate declined from 46% in 1993 to 18.3% in 2019.

agricultural products as indicated in the previous chapter. Meanwhile, agritourism (marketed as "farm-stay" or "community-based tourism") is expanding in the Lao PDR. Agritourism allows tourists to experience life on a farm and engage in activities like trekking, rice production, planting and picking coffee beans, and visiting traditional weaving villages.

Harnessing the potential of tourism services provides an opportunity for the Lao PDR to create good jobs, especially in rural areas and among women and other disadvantaged groups. As discussed in Chapter 1, tourism has many backward linkages with the agriculture sector, providing the potential to absorb excess labor in rural areas and encourage the production of higher valued-added agriculture goods and related products. In addition to increasing income for those directly employed in the tourism sector, this will generate multiplier effects for the rest of the economy and contribute toward inclusive growth.

Unfortunately, tourism is one of the worst affected sectors by the ongoing COVID-19 pandemic. The Lao PDR has been relatively successful in controlling the spread of the virus by implementing swift lockdown measures as soon as the first few cases were reported. The priority right now is to adopt appropriate policies for COVID-19 vaccine procurement, delivery, and communication to control the spread of the virus and restore confidence to restart travel and tourism. In the meantime, tourism enterprises will require support and assistance to survive the crisis and quickly bounce back when travel restrictions are slowly lifted.

The following are recommendations to implement immediately and in the short term:

1. **Provide financial support to tourism enterprises and linked businesses.** The ADB survey of Lao PDR tourism enterprises showed that the majority of them are small and will be unable to endure the protracted COVID-19 crisis. Most tourism enterprises are already struggling to stay afloat; about half of them temporarily closed in May 2020, while 83% said they would be forced to temporarily close if the crisis continued. About 70% of the surveyed enterprises had already reduced employees by around 38% in May 2020. The tourism enterprises will require financial assistance in the form of tax relief, low interest loans, and conditional cash transfers to stay in business. About 59% of enterprises in the ADB survey said they would apply for the government-established low-interest loan program for small and medium-sized enterprises (SMEs). The surveyed

enterprises most favored government policy interventions in the form of tax relief (85%) and cash transfers (69%). Similarly, lowering value-added tax from 10% to 5% has been requested by owners of hotels and restaurants and other tourism-related businesses (Vientiane Times 2021a). However, the government should also pay attention to expenditure efficiency and gradually improve the fiscal situation. Linked businesses affected by the closure of tourism enterprises should likewise be given the same support, such as farmers; transport service providers; small commercial establishments and market vendors; and those that provide associated services like cleaners, guides, and temporary and part-time workers in accommodations and food establishments.

2. **Restart the travel and tourism sector.** In 2019, domestic travelers totaled 2.3 million, while outbound trips among a population of only 7 million amounted to more than 2.6 million. In mid-2020 inter-provincial travel within the Lao PDR was allowed, and by the end of the year domestic travelers totaled 1.58 million (MICT 2020). Domestic tourism has the potential to reduce the impact of the reduction in international visitors and lead recovery of the tourism sector. To stimulate domestic travel when it is safe to travel again, local destinations and travel products can be promoted by waiving fees of tourist attractions and encouraging hotels, airlines, and tour operators to develop and advertise travel packages at reasonable prices. Similar programs have already been launched in neighboring Viet Nam and Thailand (Minh 2020; The Nation Thailand 2020). The Lao Thiao Laos (Lao Visit Laos) marketing program launched under public–private partnership was contributing to tourism recovery in 2020.

    Regional travel is likely to resume before long-haul travel. Fortunately, the Lao PDR is already a popular destination among visitors from neighboring countries. Only three countries (Thailand, the PRC, and Viet Nam) account for over 85% of arrivals and 55% of tourist spending. Vaccination programs currently being rolled out in the Lao PDR and neighboring countries are making good progress and should be accelerated.[38] Government, in coordination with the private sector, should plan for a safe and managed reopening to select international markets, starting with the critical neighboring markets. While domestic tourism and travel bubbles

---

[38] About 13% of the population in the Lao PDR had received at least one dose of vaccine in July 2021. The Ministry of Health is planning to vaccinate at least 50% of the population by the end of 2021. The PRC provided an additional 300,000 Doses of COVID-19 Vaccine to the Lao PDR (Sengpaseuth 2021). And neighboring countries like Thailand and Viet Nam started their COVID-19 Vaccination Program in Feb 2021 (Thanthong-Knight 2021, Hai 2021).

with its neighbors may not recover pre–COVID-19 levels of arrivals and spending, they may be able to save thousands of jobs and prevent many enterprises from going out of business.

3. **Adopt transparent, effective, and clearly communicated health and safety protocols and travel policy.** Domestic travel and regional travel bubbles will require transparent and evidence-based health and safety protocols and a clear communication strategy to inspire confidence among travelers. As expressed in the ADB 2020 survey, many tourism enterprises strongly support improved COVID-19 screening at borders and improved COVID-19 testing for the general population. Although travel bubbles are challenging to prepare and maintain in a fast-changing environment and with resurgence of infections highly possible, efficient cooperation and harmonization of health and safety protocols could make them viable. It is imperative to adapt travel restrictions and safety protocols in line with evolving developments of the COVID-19 pandemic to ensure they remain relevant and effective in deflecting public health threats. This would include travel and quarantine policy for vaccinated travelers. Over the long term, the Lao PDR will need to invest more heavily in modernizing health-care facilities and training medical professionals.

International tourism will become even more competitive once the pandemic subsides and international borders start to reopen. It is critical that the Lao PDR continues to invest in tourism infrastructure and services, as recommended below, so that it is able to attract high-spending tourists. More importantly, to fully benefit from the expansion of tourism services, linkages between tourism and other sectors, particularly agriculture, should be strengthened. Investments in rural infrastructure, research and development, and extension services are crucial to modernize the agriculture sector and achieve more inclusive growth.

Recommendations to strengthen the linkages between the tourism and agriculture sectors in the medium and long term are as follows:

1. **Invest in human capital development.** The Lao PDR must continue to strengthen human capital so that Lao workers can innovate, deliver higher-value tourism services, rebuild public confidence to travel post–COVID-19, and manage growth sustainably. Increasing investments in education and skills development in tourism are necessary to address the skills gaps identified in the ADB survey. The establishment of the Lao

National Institute for Tourism and Hospitality (LANITH) is a welcome development that will help address the lack of qualified educational institutions and training centers for tourism. However, further support is needed for LANITH to provide international-level training programs that respond to the dynamic needs of the tourism sector. Special attention should be given to developing managerial and digital skills at beginner and expert levels. In addition, training programs should be made accessible by increasing the number of training centers and promoting approaches such as on-the-job training and blended (online and face-to-face) learning methods. The government should engage regularly with tourism enterprises, particularly micro, small, and medium-sized enterprises, to extend the necessary support for staff development. Support should include the establishment of effective recruitment and training practices and collaboration with training institutions. Based on the AGRO Matrix in Chapter 1, this recommendation falls under the sociocultural–human dimension. Among the general recommendations is advancing training and expertise in the agricultural value chains with the aim of enhancing equity.

2. **Assist tourism enterprises and agribusinesses to acquire digital connectivity.** In the Lao PDR, e-commerce development has been largely constrained by the lack of reliable and affordable internet service providers. E-commerce remains in a development phase and more specific e-commerce laws are still under consideration. The current pandemic has highlighted the need for the country to invest in and expedite the development of its digital infrastructure to keep up with the evident shift of consumer behavior toward e-commerce. Moreover, the crisis has created opportunities for the use of various digital platforms to innovate and design creative means to get the economy running despite the lockdowns.

    The agriculture sector was part of the "e-strategy" developed to help boost demand for Lao products and services through domestic value chains. The platform links together food value chain players alongside local government units and entrepreneurs, through the use of mobile e-market services that are compliant with the government's protocols on COVID-19. Through fintech solutions, local government units are also able to monitor prices of food items and basic household commodities during the pandemic.

    Digitalization brings opportunities for tourism enterprises to expand their market and improve competitiveness and productivity. In the

ADB survey, enterprises with web presence are associated with higher levels of occupancy. However, many micro, small, and medium-sized tourism enterprises have limited access to knowledge and skills, finance, and infrastructure. Traditional business owners may have an aversion to new technology or may perceive it as risky and not beneficial. This can be managed by doing demonstration projects that provide hands-on experience to raise awareness on the benefits of digital technology. Lack of resources to engage information technology experts can be mitigated by hiring experts on a short-term basis and upskilling existing staff. Social media, like Facebook and Instagram, are effective and inexpensive avenues to communicate with the target audience. Access to digital infrastructure, such as high-speed internet, can be made possible in collaboration with private internet providers.

3. **Invest in transport infrastructure and urban services.** To enable easy access for both locals and tourists, and to move goods efficiently, it is important to invest in transport infrastructure. In particular, secondary roads and rails that connect underdeveloped and rural areas will help narrow the urban–rural divide by stimulating economic activity. The Lao PDR–PRC Railway gives the Lao PDR several advantages to expand agricultural production, marketing, and trade; and attract light manufacturing in the areas along the 414-kilometer railway from the Boten border gate in northern Louang-Namtha province to Vientiane Capital. In addition, upgrading airport facilities and services and starting more direct routes will facilitate faster growth in tourist arrivals, as evident from the rise in arrivals after upgrading of the Louangphabang airport. Urban services investments such as solid waste and wastewater management facilities, clean water supply, urban greenspace, and public markets should also be prioritized to help catalyze quality private sector tourism services investment, attract higher-spending tourists and lengthen their stay, and create opportunities for local producers to sell their goods directly to tourists and tourism enterprises.

The second and third proposals fall under the production–trade dimension of the AGRO Matrix. Among the general recommendations is to promote competitive rural enterprises. The overall objective is to promote competitiveness in line with the need to enhance productivity.

4. **Visa exemption policies and support for small and medium-sized tourism enterprises.** Policy reforms must complement investments in human capital, transportation, and digital infrastructure to

improve the business environment for tourism enterprises. To attract higher-spending visitors, the Lao PDR should expand visa exemption policies to countries with high outbound tourism expenditure. As the source market with the largest amount of tourist spending in 2019, the PRC could potentially supply more tourists to the Lao PDR if visa fees are waived, in the same way the Republic of Korea and Japan are encouraged to do so. According to the UN World Tourism Organization and the World Travel & Tourism Council, visa exemptions increase arrivals compared with electronic visa or visa on arrival policies. Case studies comparing visa exemption with other forms of visa facilitation show 5.3% higher arrivals growth when visa requirements are eliminated (UNWTO). Similarly, easing of regulatory and tax compliance requirements for SMEs and implementing modernized cross-border transport agreements to ease congestion at the Lao PDR's busy land borders are essential.

Referring to the AGRO Matrix in Chapter 1, these proposals fall under the political–institutional dimension. The primary objective is to promote good governance.

5. **Facilitate organic food production.** International tourists and even domestic consumers in the urban centers have shown preference for organic produce and better packaged food. There is significant interest for organic produce from tourism enterprises if made available in the market. Knowledge creation and knowledge sharing on the skills, practices, and technologies for organic farming are necessary to expand organic food production. Certification, labeling, and quality control measures must be put in place to ensure food safety and build consumer confidence. Current bureaucratic procedures for certification need to be streamlined and made accessible to small farmers. As discussed in Chapter 4, one approach that has worked in developing countries is the participatory guarantee system (PGS) which requires the involvement of farmers, traders, and other stakeholders in the verification process. Aside from serving as an alternative to the expensive third-party certification, this approach has resulted in greater empowerment and responsibility sharing, and improved knowledge and skills among small farmers. It has proven effective in opening organic markets to farmers while providing local organic produce to consumers more easily (Loconto, Poisot, and Santacoloma 2016). The three existing PGSs in the Lao PDR should be strengthened through regular training for farmers and alignment of standards with international guidelines such as those set by the International Federation of Organic Agriculture Movements. The PGS approach should be expanded to areas

where there is a large demand for organic food and high potential for organic farming such as in Louangphabang. Establishing a local market system involving producers, buyer groups, and tourism enterprises, along with the use of digital platforms will enable farmers to sell their produce easily. Referring to the AGRO Matrix in Chapter 1, this recommendation falls under the ecological–environmental dimension. The overall objective is to promote sustainability. Organic farming can also be the anchor of a vibrant food tourism sector.

6. **Invest in irrigation infrastructure.** Its abundant land resources give the Lao PDR enormous potential to expand its irrigated areas and boost agriculture productivity to compete in the global market. Irrigation development is the fastest and most direct way to increase crop productivity and diversify into high-value crops that have high demand in the market. The improved water availability from irrigation during the dry season allows the farming of high-yield varieties and improves the efficacy of fertilizers and pesticides to raise yields by as much as 50% on average (ADB 2018). In the past, many irrigation schemes had fallen into disrepair as a result of design flaws and limited funding for operation and maintenance because most of them were principally developed for rice cultivation with limited orientation toward other higher-value crops. New investment in irrigation will need to be properly engineered based on specific production needs and complemented with an effective extension system. Water management and firm operation and maintenance arrangements will make the country more resilient to impacts of climate change and ensure the sustainability of irrigation investments.

7. **Modernize agriculture for growth and poverty reduction.** Investment in agricultural research, development, and extension (RD&E) has proved to be one of the highest-payoff aspects of public investment. If such research is focused on improving not only yields but also the nutritional content of food staples, the resulting new varieties can boost incomes, nutrition, and health in farm households, as well as raise food self-sufficiency and lower food prices in local markets. Modernization will require agricultural research on adapting high-yielding crop varieties to local conditions and ensuring the supply of complementary modern inputs, such as chemical fertilizer and pesticides, rural credit, and access to rural electricity, in order to create a sizable marketable surplus and entice farmers to shift to more commercially oriented production. RD&E on improving the quality of cash crops, such as coffee, tea, and other crops, in which the Lao PDR has comparative advantage and established ready markets abroad, can also generate high returns.

Like the second and third proposals, the sixth and seventh proposals fall under the production–trade dimension of the AGRO Matrix. The tenor of the proposals is aligned with the general recommendation to promote competitive rural enterprises in order to enhance agricultural productivity.

References

Anderson, K. 1998. Are Resource-Abundant Economies Disadvantaged?. *Australian Journal of Agricultural and Resource Economics.* 42 (1). pp. 1–23.

Anderson, K. and W. Martin, eds. 2009. *Distortions to Agricultural Incentives in Asia.* Washington, DC: World Bank.

Anderson, K. and S. Ponnusamy. 2019. Structural Transformation to Manufacturing and Services: The Role of Trade. *Asian Development Review.* 36 (2). September. Manila: ADB.

Annim, S. and R. Gaiha. 2012. Crop Returns, Prices, Credit and Poverty in Lao PDR. *Brooks World Poverty Institute Working Paper.* 170. Manchester: Brooks World Poverty Institute.

Asian Development Bank (ADB). 2017a. *Lao PDR: Accelerating Structural Transformation for Inclusive Growth.* Country Diagnostic Study. Manila. https://www.adb.org/publications/lao-pdr-accelerating-structural-transformation-inclusive-growth.

_____. 2017b. *Tourism Sector Assessment, Strategy, and Road Map for Cambodia, Lao People's Democratic Republic, Myanmar, and Viet Nam (2016–2018).* Manila.

_____. 2018. *Agriculture, Natural Resources, and Rural Development Sector Assessment, Strategy, and Road Map: Lao PDR.* Manila.

_____. 2019. *Policies for High Quality, Safe, and Sustainable Food Supply in the Greater Mekong Subregion.* Manila. https://www.adb.org/publications/food-supply-policies-gms.

_____. 2020a. Modernizing Agriculture and Rural Development. Chapter 4 in *Asia's Journey to Prosperity: Policy, Market, and Technology over 50 Years.* Manila.

_____. 2020b. ADB Approves $20 Million to Support Lao PDR's Emergency Response to COVID-19. News Release. Manila.

_____. 2021. *Asian Development Outlook 2021*. Manila.

Association of Southeast Asian Nations (ASEAN). 2013. *ASEAN Mutual Recognition Arrangement (MRA) on Tourism Professionals Handbook*. Jakarta. https://www.asean.org/storage/images/2013/economic/handbook%20mra%20tourism_opt.pdf.

_____. 2015. ASEAN Tourism Strategic Plan 2016–2025. https://www.asean.org/storage/2012/05/ATSP-2016-2025.pdf.

ASEAN National Tourism Organization. 2013. *Farm Stay Retreats in Southeast Asia*. https://www.visitsoutheastasia.travel/activity/farm-stay-retreats-in-southeast-asia/.

Balassa, B. 1965. Trade Liberalization and "Revealed" Comparative Advantage. *Manchester School of Economics and Social Sciences*. 33 (2). pp. 90–124.

Baldwin, R. 2016. *The Great Convergence: Information Technology and the New Globalization*. Cambridge, MA and London: Harvard University Press.

_____. 2019. *The Globotics Upheaval: Globalization, Robotics and the Future of Work*. New York: Oxford University Press.

Baumüller, H. and K. Lazarus. 2012. Agribusiness Investments in Lao PDR: Opportunities and Challenges for Poverty Reduction. Technical Report. https://www.researchgate.net/publication/299352111_Agribusiness_Investments_in_Laos_PDR_Opportunities_and_Challenges_for_Poverty_Reduction.

Constantinescu, C., A. Mattoo, and M. Ruta. 2018. Trade in Developing East Asia: How It Has Changed and Why It Matters. *Policy Research Working Paper*. No. 8533. Washington, DC: World Bank.

Corden, W. M. 1984. Booming Sector and Dutch Disease Economics: Survey and Consolidation. *Oxford Economic Papers*. 36 (3). pp. 359–80.

Economic Research Institute for ASEAN and East Asia (ERIA). 2019. Agriculture and Food Processing. In M. Ambashi, ed. Development Strategy of Five Selected Sectors in the Lao People's Democratic Republic. *ERIA Research Report*. FY2018 No. 7. Jakarta.

Economic and Social Commission for Asia and the Pacific (ESCAP) and United Nations Conference on Trade and Development (UNCTAD). 2019. Laos Trade Facilitation: Current on Cross Border Transport Connectivity Infrastructure. Workshop on Promoting Structural Economic Transformation in Asian-Pacific Landlocked Developing Countries. Thailand. 4–7 November.

Fleischer, A. and D. Felsenstein. 2000. Support for Rural Tourism: Does It Make a Difference?. *Annals of Tourism Research.* 27 (4). pp. 1007–1024.

Fong, L. H. N., R. Law, and B. H. Ye. 2020. Outlook of Tourism Recovery Amid an Epidemic: Importance of Outbreak Control by the Government. *Annals of Tourism Research.* Elsevier. https://doi.org/10.1016/j.annals.2020.102951.

Food and Agriculture Organization of the United Nations (FAO). 2020. Special R–port – 2019 FAO/WFP Crop and Food Security Assessment Mission to the Lao People's Democratic Republic. Rome. https://doi.org/10.4060/ca8392en.

_____. 2018. Country Gender Assessment of Agriculture and the Rural Sector in the Lao People's Democratic Republic. Vientiane.

Freebairn, J. 2015. Mining Booms and the Exchange Rate. *Australian Journal of Agricultural and Resource Economics.* 59 (4). pp. 533–48.

GIZ Agriculture & Food Cluster E-Magazine (GIZ). 2017a. Phutawen Farm: The New Hub of Sustainable Agro-Tourism in Lao PDR. Bangkok. https://www.asean-agrifood.org/phutawen-farm-the-new-hub-of-sustainable-agro-tourism-in-lao-pdr/ (accessed 11 April 2020).

_____. 2017b. Sector Skills Study for the Agriculture and Food Processing Sectors and Value Chain Analyses for Selected Sub-Sectors of the Agriculture and Food Processing Sectors. Vocational Education in Lao PDR Project Report. Vientiane Capital: GIZ.

Government of the Lao People's Democratic Republic (Lao PDR). 2013. *Tourism Law.* No. 32/NA. Vientiane Capital.

Government of the People's Republic of China (PRC). 2018. National Strategic Plan for Rural Vitalization, 2018–2022. Beijing.

Hai, V. 2021. Vietnam to Receive 5 Mln Covid-19 Vaccine Doses in February. *VNExpress.* February 15. https://e.vnexpress.net/news/news/vietnam-to-receive-5-mln-covid-19-vaccine-doses-in-february-4235752.html.

Hall, C. M., L. Sharples, R. Mitchell, N. Macionis, and B. Cambourne, eds. 2003. *Food Tourism Around the World: Development, Management and Markets.* Oxford: Elsevier Ltd.

Hepburn, E. 2008. Agritourism as a Viable Strategy for Economic Diversification: A Case Study Analysis of Policy Options for the Bahamas. *All Dissertations.* 313. https://tigerprints.clemson.edu/all_dissertations/313.

Hoppe, M., S. Zoriya, A. Reichhuber, K. Sarayath, W. Loundu, and S. Solitham. 2018. *Commercialization of Rice and Vegetables Value Chain in Lao PDR: Status and Prospects*. Washington, DC: World Bank.

Horwath HTL. 2019. Luxury & Upper Upscale Hotel Market Overview: Louangphabang. Singapore.

Inter-American Institute for Cooperation in Agriculture (IICA). 2015. Report on the Meetings of Ministers of Agriculture and the AGRO 2003–2015 Plan for Agriculture and Rural Life in the Americas. San Jose, Costa Rica. http://repositorio.iica.int/bitstream/handle/11324/4011/(WD-378)%20Report%20on%20the%20Meetings%20of%20Ministers%20of%20Agriculture%20and%202003-2015%20Agro%20Plan.pdf;jsessionid=D0F12DD1BA8A6FA99237B678AC63656F?sequence=1.

International Food Policy Research Institute (IFPRI). 2019. *2019 Global Food Policy Report*. Washington, DC. https://www.globalhungerindex.org/pdf/en/2019/Lao-PDR.pdf.

Keola, S. 2019. Geographical Simulation Analysis of the Lao-Chinese High-Speed Railway. In Japan External Trade Organization. *EEC Development and Transport Facilitation Measures in Thailand and the Development Strategies by the Neighboring Countries*. Bangkok: JETRO.

Khanal, B. R. 2011. An Economic Analysis of the Lao PDR Tourism Industry. PhD dissertation. Lincoln University.

Laborde, D., T. Lallemant, K. McDougal, C. Smaller and F. Traore. 2018. *Transforming Agriculture in Africa and Asia: What Are the Priorities?*. Geneva: International Institute for Sustainable Development and Washington, DC: IFPRI.

Lao Statistics Bureau. 2014. Poverty Profile in Lao PDR: Poverty Report from the Lao Consumption and Expenditure Survey 2012/13. Vientiane.

Lao Statistics Bureau and the World Bank. 2020. *Poverty Profile in Lao PDR: Poverty Report from the Lao Expenditure and Consumption Survey 2018–2019*. Vientiane: Lao Statistics Bureau. http://pubdocs.worldbank.org/en/923031603135932002/Lao-PDR-Poverty-Profile-Report-ENG.pdf.

Leamer, E. E. 1987. Paths of Development in the Three-Factor, n-Good General Equilibrium Model. *Journal of Political Economy*. 95 (5). pp. 961–99.

Loconto, A., A. S. Poisot, and P. Santacoloma, eds. 2016. *Innovative Markets for Sustainable Agriculture – How Innovations in Market Institutions Encourage Sustainable Agriculture in Developing Countries.* Rome: FAO and Institut National de la Recherche Agronomique (INRA).

Luxembourg Development Cooperating Agency. 2018. *Enterprise Survey of Employment and Skills in Lao PDR: Research Findings and Employment Projections, 2018–2023.* Vientiane.

Market Watch. 2020. Online Travel Market: Global Industry Analysis Outlook by Size, Share, Growth, Trends and Forecast 2020-2023. Press release. 29 October. https://www.marketwatch.com/press-release/online-travel-market-global-industry-analysis-outlook-by-size-share-growth-trends-and-forecast-2020-2023-2020-10-29.

McKinley, T. 2010. Inclusive Growth Criteria and Indicators: An Inclusive Growth Index for Diagnosis of Country Progress. *ADB Sustainable Development Working Paper Series.* Manila: ADB.

McKinsey & Company. 2018. *Chinese Tourists: Dispelling the Myths: An In-Depth Look at China's Outbound Tourist Market.* Hong Kong, China.

Mekong Tourism Coordinating Office. 2016. *Greater Mekong Subregion Tourism Sector Strategy 2016–2025.* Bangkok.

Menon, J. and P. G. Warr. 2013. The Lao Economy: Capitalizing on Natural Resource Exports. *Asian Economic Policy Review.* 8 (1). pp. 70–89.

Minh. V. 2020. "Vietnamese People Travel in Vietnam" Program Kicks Off. *Hanoi Times.* 12 May. http://hanoitimes.vn/vietnamese-people-travel-in-vietnam-program-kicks-off-312047.html.

Ministry of Agriculture and Forestry. 2014. *Lao PDR: Lao Census of Agriculture 2010/11 – Analyses of Selected* Themes. Vientiane.

_____. 2015a. Development Strategy of the Crop Sector 2025 and Vision 2030. Vientiane.

_____. 2015b. Strategic Plan for National Organic Agriculture Development 2025 and Vision Toward 2030. Vientiane.

_____. 2020. Agricultural Statistics Year Book 2019. Vientiane.

Ministry of Information, Culture and Tourism (MICT). 2014. 2014 Statistical Report on Tourism in Laos. Vientiane.

_____. 2015. 2015 Statistical Report on Tourism in Laos. Vientiane.

_____. 2016. 2016 Statistical Report on Tourism in Laos. Vientiane.

_____. 2017. 2017 Statistical Report on Tourism in Laos. Vientiane.

_____. 2018. 2018 Statistical Report on Tourism in Laos. Vientiane.

_____. 2019. 2019 Statistical Report on Tourism in Laos. Vientiane.

_____. 2020. 2020 Statistical Report on Tourism in Laos. Vientiane.

Namvong, S. 2020. Blog 1 COVID-19 in Lao PDR: Impacts on Agriculture and Rural Advisory Services. APIRAS Network. 7 May. https://apiras. net/blog-1-covid-19-in-lao-pdr-impacts-on-agriculture-and-rural-advisory-services/#.

National Statistics Centre, Committee for Planning and Investment. 2005. *1975–2005 Basic Statistics: The Socio-Economic Development of Lao PDR*. Vientiane.

_____. 2014. *Poverty Profile in Lao PDR: Poverty Report for the Lao Consumption and Expenditure Survey, 2012–2013*. Vientiane.

_____. 2018. *2017 Statistics Yearbook*. Vientiane.

Oraboune, S. 2008. Agricultural Commercialization, A Strategic Direction for Rural Farmers to Overcome Poverty in Lao PDR. In M. Suzuki, ed. *Perspective of Lao Economic Development – Impact of AFTA Scheme*. pp. 75–130. JICA and NERI. https://www.researchgate. net/publication/318489506_Agricultural_Commercialization_A_Strategic_Direction_for_Rural_Farmers_to_Overcome_Poverty_in_Lao_PDR.

Parvathi, P. 2018. Does Mixed Crop-Livestock Farming Lead to Less Diversified Diets Among Farmholders? Evidence from Laos. *Agricultural Economics*. 49 (4). pp. 497–509.

Rodrik, D. 2018. New Technologies, Global Value Chains, and Developing Countries. *NBER Working Paper*. 25164. Cambridge, MA.

Savankham, F. 2020a. Laos to Enter Lockdown Starting March 30. *The Laotian Times*. 29 March. https://laotiantimes. com/2020/03/29/laos-to-enter-full-lockdown-startingmarch-30/.

_____. 2020b. Laos to Resume Domestic Flights, Schools, Other Restrictions Eased. *The Laotian Times*. https://opendevelopmentmekong.net/news/laos-to-resume-domestic-flights-schools-other-restrictions-eased/.

Schoenweger, O. and A. Ullenberg. 2010. *Foreign Direct Investment (FDI) in Land in the Lao PDR*. Eschborn: GTZ.

Schoenweger, O., A. Heinimann, M. Epprecht, J. Lu, and P. Thalongsengchanh. 2012. *Concessions and Leases in the Lao PDR: Taking Stock of Land Investments*. Bern: Geographica Bernensia. DOI: 10.13140/RG.2.1.3501.7047.

Sengpaseuth, P. 2021. China Provides Additional 300,000 Doses of COVID-19 Vaccine. *Vientiane Times*. 9 February. https://vientianetimes.org.la/freeContent/FreeConten_China_27.php.

Slocum, S. L. and K. R. Curtis. 2018. *Food and Agricultural Tourism: Theory and Best Practice*. New York: Routledge.

Surana, S. 2016. In Laos, a Haven for Tubing Offers More Peace, Less Partying. *The New York Times*. https://www.nytimes.com/2016/10/02/travel/vang-vieng-laos-river-tubing-haven-offers-more-peace.html%20;%20https://edition.cnn.com/travel/article/vang-vieng-laos-adventure/index.html.

The Nation Thailand. 2020. "We Love Thailand" to Stimulate Domestic Demand. 4 May. https://www.nationthailand.com/news/30387237.

Thanthong-Knight, R. 2021. Thailand to Start COVID-19 Vaccination Program from Feb 14. *Bloomberg*. 25 January. https://www.bloomberg.com/news/articles/2021-01-25/thailand-set-to-start-covid-19-vaccination-program-from-feb-14.

United Nations Conference on Trade and Development (UNCTAD). 2012. Lao's Organic Agriculture: 2012 Update. Project Report on Enhancing Sustainable Tourism, Clean Production and Export Capacity in Lao People's Democratic Republic. https://sites.google.com/site/organiclao/national-update.

_____. 2014. *Enhancing Backward Linkages between Tourism and Other Sectors in Lao People's Democratic Republic*. Geneva. https://unctad.org/en/PublicationsLibrary/ditcted2014d4_en.pdf.

_____. 2016. Lao Government Sees Bright Future in Organic Farming. 8 July. https://unctad.org/news/laos-government-sees-bright-future-organic-farming.

_____. 2020. *Lao People's Democratic Republic: Sustainable Commercialization in the Coffee Value Chain*. Geneva.

United Nations Department of Economic and Social Affairs, Population Division (UNDESA). 2019. *World Population Prospects 2019*. Online Edition. Rev. 1. New York.

United Nations Development Programme (UNDP). 2012. Nam Ha Ecotourism Project: Lao People's Democratic Republic. *UNDP Equator Initiative Case Study Series*. New York.

United Nations World Tourism Organization (UNWTO). 2014. *Visa Openness Report 2014*. Madrid.

_____. 2018. *UNWTO Tourism Highlights 2018*. Madrid.

_____. 2019. *Tourism and the Sustainable Development Goals*. Madrid.

_____. 2020. Global Guidelines to Re-Start Tourism. Madrid.

_____. 2021. World Tourism Barometer. Madrid.

United Nations World Tourism Organization (UNWTO) and World Travel & Tourism Council (WTTC). 2014. *The Impact of Visa Facilitation in ASEAN Member States*. Madrid.

United States Department of Commerce, Bureau of the Census. 2013. American Community Survey 1-Year Estimates. Washington, DC.

Vientiane Times. 2021a. Ministry Seeks to Bolster Tourism through Lao Thiao Laos. 5 March.

_____. 2021b. Laos Bolsters Asean Efforts to Revive Tourism. 5 February.

_____. 2021c. Second Round of Covid-19 Vaccinations to Begin this Month. 3 March. https://www.vientianetimes.org.la/freeContent/ FreeConten_ Second_43.php.

Warr, P. G., J. Menon, and A. A. Yusuf. 2012. Poverty Impacts of Natural Resource Revenues. *Journal of Asian Economics*. 23 (4). pp. 442–53.

Warr, P. G., S. Rasphone, and J. Menon. 2018. Two Decades of Rising Inequality and Declining Poverty in the Lao People's Democratic Republic. *Asian Economic Journal*. 32 (2). pp. 165–85.

World Bank. 2015. Drivers of Poverty Reduction in Lao PDR. Lao PDR Poverty Policy Notes. Washington, DC.

_____. 2018a. *Commercialization of Rice and Vegetable Value Chains in Lao PDR: Status and Prospects*. Washington, DC.

_____. 2018b. Digital Connectivity in Lao PDR Lagging Behind Peers: A Short Assessment with Policy Recommendations to Catch Up. Washington, DC.

_____. 2020. *Lao People's Democratic Republic Poverty Assessment 2020: Catching Up and Falling Behind*. Washington, DC. https:// openknowledge.worldbank.org/handle/10986/34528.

World Economic Forum. 2019. *The Travel and Tourism Competitiveness Report 2019*. Geneva.

World Food Programme. 2020. Rapid Assessment of Food Security and Agriculture in Lao PDR. Vientiane.

World Trade Organization (WTO). 2018. *Tariff Profiles 2018*. Geneva.

_____. 2019. World Tariff Profiles 2019. Geneva. www.wto.org/statistics.

_____. 2014. *The Impact of Visa Facilitation in ASEAN Member States.* Madrid.

World Travel & Tourism Council (WTTC). 2020. Southeast Asia Tourism Recovery Policy Dialogue: Rebuilding Economic and Social Benefits – Re-inspiring Traveler Confidence. London.

_____. 2021. *Lao Economic Impact Report 2021.* London.

Yap, J. 2017. Everything You Need to Know about the Laos-China Railway. *The Laotian Times.* 20 February. https://laotiantimes.com/2017/02/20/everything-you-need-to-know-laos-china-railway/.

Yusuf, S. and P. Kumar. 2018. Playing to Strength Growth Strategy for Small Agrarian Economies in Africa. *Policy Research Working Paper.* No. 8543. Washington, DC: World Bank.

www.ingramcontent.com/pod-product-compliance
Lightning Source LLC
Chambersburg PA
CBHW082349230326
41599CB00058BA/7185